THE CONSERVATIVES' ECONOMIC POLICY

THE CONSERVATIVES' ECONOMIC POLICY

Grahame Thompson

CROOM HELM

London • Sydney • Dover, New Hampshire

©1986 Grahame F Thompson
Croom Helm Ltd, Provident House, Burrell Row,
Beckenham, Kent BR3 1AT

Croom Helm Australia Pty Ltd, Suite 4, 6th Floor,
64-76 Kippax Street, Surry Hills, NSW 2010, Australia

British Library Cataloguing in Publication Data
Thompson, Grahame
    The Conservatives' economic policy.
    1. Great Britain – Economic policy – 1945-
    I. Title
    330.941'0858   HC256.6

    ISBN 0-7099-2480-1
    ISBN 0-7099-2484-4 Pbk

Croom Helm, 51 Washington Street, Dover,
New Hampshire 03820, USA

Library of Congress Cataloging in Publication Data
Thompson, Grahame.
    The conservative's economic policy, 1979–1984.

    Includes index.
        1. Great Britain–economic policy–1945-
    2. Great Britain–economic conditions–1945-
    3. Great Britain–politics and government–1979-
    I. Title.
    HC256.6.T48   1986   338.941   86-6225
    ISBN 0-7099-2480-1
    ISBN 0-7099-2484-4 (pbk.)

Printed and bound in Great Britain by Mackays of Chatham Ltd, Kent

CONTENTS

Contents

TABLES AND FIGURES

Tables and Figures

Tables and Figures

ACKNOWLEDGEMENTS

I would like to thank a number of people who have
read parts of this book and commented on it during
its short production period. In particular, Jim
Tomlinson, Neil Kay, Mike Williams, Alan Gillie and
Stephen Culliford. An earlier version of Chapter 7
was presented at the 1984 annual Conference of
Socialist Economists meeting in Manchester. I thank
the participants for their comments. Finally, the
secretaries of the Faculty of Social Sciences at
the Open University more or less collectively
assembled the typescript while other business was
pressing. Ann Boomer, Gloria Channing and Iris
Manzi in particular deserve my gratitude.

Chapter 1

INTRODUCTION

When Sir Geoffrey Howe made his first Budget speech
in 1979 as the new Chancellor of the Exchequer he
was able to lay out four main principles on which
the Conservative Government's economic strategy was
to be built:

. the need to strengthen incentives, by
  allowing people to keep more of what they
  earn, so that hard work, talent and
  ability are properly rewarded;
. the need to enlarge freedom of choice for
  the individual by reducing the role of the
  State;
. the need to reduce the burden of financing
  the public sector, so as to leave room for
  commerce and industry to prosper;
. and the need to ensure, so far as
  possible, that those who take part in
  collective bargaining understand the
  consequences of their actions - for that
  is the way to promote a proper sense of
  responsibility. People had to understand
  and accept that the only basis for real
  increases in wages and salaries was an
  increase in national production. Higher
  pay without higher productivity could only
  lead to higher inflation and unemployment.
  (Quoted by Leon Brittan in Kay 1982 p.9).

Coupled with the main objective of reducing
inflation these principles became enshrined in a
philosophy that seems to have sustained the
Conservative Party's economic strategy ever since
they took office in 1979. Leon Brittan, formerly
Chief Secretary to the Treasury and a firm
supporter of Margaret Thatcher's 'new line'

described these principles as offering a radical new beginning (p.10). Indeed this theme of the radicalism of the new government was not something simply celebrated by the Conservative Right. It was a theme readily embraced by the Left as well. A new era had been launched in 1974, it was argued, when Mrs Thatcher took over the Conservative Party Leadership, and 'Thatcherism' as a combination of 'populist authoritarianism' and a belief in the 'social market economy' came firmly to roost after her 1979 election victory (Hall and Jacques 1983). Consensus on all fronts was broken. A new direction for the economy and society was in order.

Whilst it might be objected that these kinds of comments represent the typical claims expected from the extremes of the political spectrum, in fact they are not simply to be found there. Even so called moderate or middle ground opinion has promoted these types of arguments, though perhaps with greater qualification. Thus Victor Keegan in his recent book on Margaret Thatcher's first government (Keegan 1984), echos J.K. Galbraith's remarks in suggesting that the UK was subject to an experiment in 'evangelical monetarism' over the period 1979 to 1983. Keegan wants to pitch this against the virtues of a rather orthodox Keynesianism, the re-installation of which he sees as offering a real salvation for the UK's depressed economic condition. In addition the influential Brookings Institution partly endorsed the general view when introducing an important paper by two of the most able critics of the Conservative Government's economic policy. The editors of the Brookings Papers on Economic Activity sum up Willem Buiter and Marcus Miller's paper as follows: (No.2 1983)

> The Government of Margaret Thatcher has drastically altered the conduct of economic policy in the United Kingdom. She has changed the ultimate objectives of policy, the way in which policy instruments are applied, and the relation between the government and organized labour. Taken together these actions constitute a revolution in economic policy making. (pIX).

In fact Buiter and Miller's analysis offers a more qualified and cautious assessment than their editors suggest, but still along the lines of the dominant 'radical change' type of argument. Their position on the macro-economic stance of the economy over the period of the Conservatives' first adminstration is discussed in Chapter 2. Here a number of important reservations to their position are offered while generally endorsing it with respect to fiscal stance and the form and effectiveness of monetary policy. However the implications and consequences drawn from this assessment are quite different to theirs and go to undermine the way they discuss the construction of economic objectives and the relationship between economic theory and economic policy.

By and large the Buiter and Miller and Keegan type critiques - as well as those emanating further from the Left - are pitched at the aggregative, macro-level of the economy. They do not look closely and in detail at the more micro aspects of government intervention - at industrial policy and de-nationalization, at personal incentives and taxation, at an incomes policy and the like. In Chapters 5, 6 and 7 below the analysis is focused on these areas to integrate them into a more complete and overall asssessment.

In general terms this book concentrates upon the central aspects of the Conservative Party's economic policies in an attempt to disentangle the rhetoric from the realities of economic policy making and its implementation. The idea is not to take the exaggerated claims of either the Right or the Left at their face value but rather to assess carefully the character of any changes so far wrought in the mechanisms of the economy. This will involve an analysis of both the changing objectives of government policy and the constraints and obstacles this has encountered, as well as a look at some of the economic theory that has been suggested in support of the changed approach to the economy. Whilst it is intended that this examination should be conducted in as critical a manner as possible it is not the objective of this book to suggest an alternative package of theoretical or policy options. In addition the nature of the 'animal' being dealt with here - i.e. a modern integrated industrial and financial economy - means that the discussion will of necessity be selective rather than comprehensive. The focus will be upon the four main issues raised in Sir Geoffrey Howe's speech mentioned above along with the central issue of inflation. These will be examined in the context of the question of a radical change or otherwise in the practices of economic management and regulation that have characterized the UK economy over the period 1979-1984.

The period over which this analysis is focused is important in limiting the purview of the arguments developed. It takes the five years between mid 1979 (the time the Conservatives gained office) to mid 1985 as the focus for discussion. This pushes it well past the important March 1984 Budget. Clearly events are moving fast in the areas looked at in detail in the chapters below and are likely to maintain their momentum in the medium term. This means that the analysis offered can only constitute a particular 'interim' one. As things progress the arguments advanced will no doubt require some qualification. Such is the difficulty of writing books with a conjunctional or policy focus. What the book offers however is an assessment of what has happened over the period which hopefully sustains a more adequate and comprehensive approach to the Conservatives' economic policy making than has so far emerged in the literature.

Although the emphasis in this account is upon what has happened in a policy context, the book is not simply about economic policy. Indeed at certain points the object of focus switches to elements of economic theory that have also come to the fore during the period from the mid 1970s. With respect to this aspect the period dealt with has to be slightly longer. In fact some of the theoretical developments reviewed have a very long pedigree, and where it seems appropriate to refer to this such reference is made. This happens to be the case with the so called 'rational expectations' revolution, which is raised and discussed in Chapter 3. Most contemporary accounts of this issue concentrate on Muth's article of 1961. But this formed the culmination of a rather lengthy discussion of expectation formation that appeared in American journals in the late 1950s and which was specifically focused around the formation of agricultural prices. This original and limited purview of the discussion is raised in Chapter 3 which argues, as a result, that a much more differentiated view of expectations formation be taken.

The point about a slightly wider brief being taken for the discussion of expectation formation serves to introduce a more general point about the approach adopted here. At times the analysis presses for a rather 'open' stance towards such areas as the general analysis of markets and the question of economic rationality, incentives, etc. The burden of these positions is to argue for a more differentiated approach to be undertaken towards economic analysis and the economy so analysed than is often the case in more orthodox accounts. In no way does this represent a comprehensive critical account of such orthodoxies but it is mentioned here to register an underlying difference of approach, which surfaces at times in relation to the arguments being assessed.

The reference to Muth's analysis of expectation formation above, also raises another preliminary point. Clearly this represents a form of economic theorization about which much has been written and indeed about which much more could be said. The remarks in Chapter 3 about this add very little to what are probably already well known positions and are only designed to be comprehensible to a relatively unfamiliar reader in these matters. Similarly with other general theoretical stances adopted by the 'New Right' as it is termed, such as supply-side economics or Hayekian neo-liberalism as applied to economic matters. The analysis here looks at these only 'in passing' as it were, to highlight some of their more pertinent policy suggestions and possible connections to the Conservative Government's approach to the economy. As we shall see these have had only a limited and uneven impact on such policy formation though they have served an important function of ideologically underpinning it.

Here we draw an important distinction between two levels of the policy making process - the level of policy 'promotion/determination' and the level of policy 'formation/implementation'. Policy 'promotion/determination' has more to do with abstract objectives that those advising the relevant policy makers may wish to promote, or even that those policy makers may themselves wish to achieve. Policy 'formation/implementation', on the other hand, describes more the resulting way in which such objectives either coincide with, juxtapose against, or become articulated with, both the instruments of policy and, perhaps more importantly, with the constraints on any actual change. Policy promotion/determination thus looks 'backwards' as it were, to the 'principles' and theoretical arguments used to justify or promote a particular piece of policy advice or course of desired action, while policy implementation/formation looks 'forward', as it were, to 'outcome' (rather than to objectives) and to the processes which intervene and 'form' the actual course taken. As we shall see these two aspects of the policy making process need have little connection in actual practical instances.

A further aspect to the question of theoretical ideas and their purview with respect to the analysis and descriptions offered in subsequent chapters, is that theory can be discussed at at least two levels here. On the one hand theoretical arguments can be pitched at an abstract level and with respect to general theories. On the other they can be focused on a more mundane, ad hoc and partial level. In the case of the problems being confronted in the book, involving as they do policy question and practical issues, this latter aspect provides the predominant focus for the analysis. The period with which this book is concernedcoincided with the rapid development of econometric models of the economy designed to test and simulate alternative policy scenarios. This has produced a very active and mushrooming economic policy 'environment' in which different forecasters argue and vie between themselves over both where the economy has got to and where it is likely to go. Table 1.1 lists the most important of the forecasting teams who make use of such econometric models. There is no space to review even the more important of these models in this book. In any case they have been comprehensively discussed in Posner (1978) and in Ormerod (1979). However a number of the more practical theoretical developments at this level, that lie behind the emergence of such models are referred to, again rather in passing, where their pertinence is useful to elaborate a point in connection with policy formation.

Table 1.1: Organizations Conducting Detailed Economic Policy Assessment of the U.K. Economy.

Henley Forecasting, London Business School, National Institute of Economic and Social Research, Treasury, Cambridge Econometrics (C.P.G.), Liverpool University, Bank of England, Data Research Inc., Staniland Hall, Oxford Economic Forecasting, Phillips and Drew, Confederation of British Industry, James Capel, Simon and Coates, Hoare Govett, Laing and Cruckshank, Grieveson Grant, Wood MacKenzie, Capel-Cure Myers, OECD.

Source: _Financial Times_ April 5 1984.

Of course these two levels of theory are not independent of one another. Rational expectations for example was something taken up in the explicit context of model building - it specifies a way of representing the inflationary process in general - but it also connects up to a way of analysing the wider role of markets as mechanisms of resource allocation and co-ordination. However for analytical purposes it is useful to separate the theory of markets in general, for instance (of which rational expectations is admittedly a part) from those aspects of theoretical model building involving an explicit reference to the construction of behavioural relationships to test and simulate various policy regimes.

In addition to these references to theoretical and 'semi-theoretical' developments, a good deal of emphasis in the chapters below is given to the changing historical features and conditions for economic calculation to take place and for such theoretical stances to emerge and to connect. Thus the approach adopted here situates the re-emergence of particular general theoretical schemes and new empirical techniques of estimation in the context of the conditions in the economy which stimulated these and 'allowed' them to appear and to take hold. Thus one of the features of the analysis is to emphasize the real conditions of the economy that provided the context in which different rationalizations for economic policy appear and are conferred with a legitimacy. In particular developments in the international economy and in financial and monetary matters are emphasized. This is not because such 'monetary' matters are any more important than developments in the economy's 'real' features, but rather because the monetary and financial features focused upon have been relatively underemphasized in most accounts, and because they constitute the immediate determinants of much of the changed approach to economic theory and policy making that has developed since the mid 1970s.

The plan of the rest of this book is as follows. The next chapter looks at the macro-economic developments broadly speaking in the context of the Conservatives' Medium Term Financial Strategy. Chapter 3 raises a number of issues concerning changes in the international context of the UK economy particularly the implications of floating exchange rates. In this context the theoretical responses to the uncertainties that floating exchange rates produced are reviewed and the whole

question of markets and their role discussed.
Chapter 4 provides a framework for moving from the
macro-environment to the micro - one in terms of
the policy promotion/determination initiatives that
the Conservatives had made. The policy formation/
implementation stage broadly speaking forms the
focus for the following three chapters. In Chapter
5 competition policy in all its facets is looked
at. This is followed by a more detailed discussion
of taxation and social security matters and
initiatives in Chapter 6. In Chapter 7 the
Conservatives' approach to industrial policy and
de-nationalization is reviewed. Finally, there is a
short concluding chapter.

In general terms this book argues _against_ a
well known or even dominant position in the debate
about the Conservative Government's economic
policy. It argues that continuities in economic
policy making are still stronger than radical
changes. It does not suggest that nothing has
changed nor that more significant radical alterations
in direction could not emerge. But it is sceptical
of the totally 'new brush' ideology that the
Conservatives have themselves floated and which has
been taken up by most commentators. The chapters
outlined above offer the reader a series of essays
on contemporary issues which go to substantiate
this claim. They are not essentially structured,
but rather, are loosely connected to this end. Thus
readers may dip into this book as they wish,
picking topics which interest them in an order
determined by themselves.

Introduction

References

Brookings Institution (1983) <u>Papers on Economic Activity</u>. No.2 Washington DC.

Hall, S. and Jacques, M. (1983) <u>The Politics of Thatcherism</u>. Laurence and Wishart, London.

Kay, J. (ed) (1982) <u>The 1982 Budget</u>. Basil Blackwell, Oxford.

Keegan, V.P. (1984) <u>Mrs Thatcher's Economic Experiment</u>. Allen Lane, London.

Muth, J. (1961) 'Rational Expectations and the Theory of Price Movements' <u>Econometrica</u>. July, pp.315-35.

Ormerod, P.A. (1979) <u>Economic Modeling</u>. Heinemann Educational Books, London.

Posner, M. (ed) (1978) <u>Demand Management</u>. Heinemann London.

Chapter 2

THE 'MEDIUM TERM FINANCIAL STRATEGY' AND MACRO-ECONOMIC
REGULATION

1.   INTRODUCTION

Perhaps the centre piece of the Conservatives'
economic strategy at a macro-economic level has
been their 'Medium Term Financial Strategy' (MTFS)
launched in March 1980 soon after they took office.
This has been paraded as an innovative financial
policy that attempts to set targets for a range of
intermediate monetary variables in the economy,
particularly those connected with the money supply
(Ms) and the Public Sector Borrowing Requirements
(PSBR).[1] The main idea here is to control the
economy largely via financial or monetary means;
fiscal or budgetary policy is allocated a secondary
position in this management framework. Formally at
least this latter aspect is subsidiary to financial
or monetary policy. This provides the main
connection to the supposed demise of Keynesianism
as a management framework and its replacement by
monetarism. Inflation became the primary policy
problem for governments and employment levels were
relegated to a secondary or 'residual' position. In
fact it was argued that 'real productive'
employment could only result from such a policy as
is made clear below. Thus what is formally
foregrounded in the strategy is the necessity to
deal with inflation (a 'monetary' phenomena) via
the instruments of monetary policy in the first
instance: namely by controlling the monetary level
of public expenditure (so called 'cash limit'
planning and monitoring the PSBR) and using the
money supply as the main targeted variable to
effect the levels of credit and money circulating
in the private economy. A Keynesian 'budgetary
policy' approach is displaced by a monetarist
'financial policy' one. Such a policy also relies

upon the characteristic monetarist assertion that there is a close, if lagged link between the money supply and the price level, and the change in the price level or inflation. Controlling the money supply thus controls inflation.

In this chapter a full scale theoretical elaboration of these ideas is not undertaken. It concentrates instead on the policy implications and problems that have arisen in the context of the Conservatives' attempts to implement such a strategy. This has formed a central plank on which the Government have staked a great deal in terms of their 'new broom' ideology. It therefore provides a crucial test for the character of this strategy. In fact the chapter argues that the reduction in inflation achieved by the Conservatives during their first five years in office had less to do with the supposed monetarism of their MTFS and more to do with the deflationary 'real' fiscal stance and accommodating tight monetary policy that they pursued, which was in turn quite compatible with an underlying Keynesian type framework.

2. THE MONEY SUPPLY AND THE PSBR

In the UK context one of the main supports for the MTFS has been the argument about the close relationship existing between the money supply and the PSBR. This relationship has been most forcefully advocated by economists initially working at the London Business School (LBS). An explanation of this can best be undertaken in the context of the 'credit counterparts' which make up the components of the money supply. These can be generated from the balance sheet identity between the assets and the liabilities of the banking system as a whole (see LBS Economic Outlook February 1980, June 1980 and October 1980). This identity can be specified and stated as follows:

$$\triangle Ms = PSBR - \triangle G_p + \triangle L_p + EF \ldots(1)$$

The equation says that a change in the money supply ($\triangle$ Ms) is equal to the PSBR, minus any change in the non-bank private sector's lending to the public sector, or the public sector's borrowing from the non-bank private sector ($\triangle$ Gp) plus any changes in the banks lending to the non-bank private sector ($\triangle$ Lp), and finally plus any net external financing (EF) which comprises net

11

borrowing and lending abroad. The items on the right of the equation are the 'credit counterparts' of the money supply appearing on the left of the equation.

The PSBR is one of the credit counterparts to the money supply shown in this equation. Thus as the concern developed with controlling inflation, and as this was increasingly theoretically linked to the control of the money supply, equation (1) offered a link between controlling inflation and controlling the PSBR. In effect it was argued that a change in the PSBR would lead to a change in the money supply which would eventually lead to a change in the price level (ie $\triangle$ PSBR $\triangle$ Ms $\triangle$P). But such a relationship between the PSBR and the money supply is not an instantaneous nor automatic one it is stressed. Any change in the PSBR could be offset by sales of public debt to the non-bank private sector ($\triangle$ Gp), by changes in bank lending to the non-bank private sector ($\triangle$ Lp) or by changes in external finance (EF), all linked together as in equation (1). What a change in the PSBR does, it is claimed, is set up a series of complicated portfolio adjustments into which various lags will be built. The movement between stock concepts and flow concepts is thus dependent upon a theory of portfolio balances and adjustments which is expressed in the appropriate behavioural equations of the econometric models used by forecasters. It is these behavioural equations that effectively convert the identity shown as equation (1) into a behavioural theory involving a chain of causation leading from the left to the right of the relationship. Given that the money supply (itself the 'cause' of inflation) is shown to be dependent, at least in part, on the PSBR, the control of inflation implies putting downward pressure on public expenditure. Thus the level of public expenditure emerged as a prime 'cause' of inflation, if indirectly via its link to the PSBR and the money supply.

In addition this equation can be used to point to another consequence of the analysis. Arguments were advanced for the idea that public expenditure 'crowded out' private expenditure. Attached to this was a further consideration, namely that public expenditure was less productive than was private expenditure. Thus it was an 'unproductive' (public) expenditure that was crowding out or displacing a more productive (private) expenditure, and this was argued to be one of the causes of the poor performance of the economy. To show formally how this argument worked we can refer once again to equation (1). Supposing we assume that the external position is constrained so that we hold EF constant. In addition let us assume that the negative item in the equation, G_p, is also held constant, i.e. that changes in the private sector lending to the public sector via Gilt purchases is also constrained in the short-run. Thus we can interpret equation (1) as:

$$\triangle Ms \quad = \quad PSBR \quad + \quad \triangle L_p \quad \ldots \ldots \ldots \ldots (2)$$

In this case, if we want to control the money supply, $\triangle Ms$, by maintaining it at a constant level for instance, the PSBR and $\triangle L_p$ - or bank lending to the private sector - are <u>substitutes</u> for one another. To increase the PSBR is to decrease lending to the private sector. Thus the PSBR 'crowds out' lending to the 'productive' private sector under these circumstances. A reduction in the PSBR could allow more bank lending to the private sector while still maintaining the money supply constant and under control.

Finally we can use equation (1) to explain the character of another theoretical development that arose in the early 1980s namely the so called 'monetary approach to the balance of payments' (MAP). It is argued that the characteristic Keynesian approach to the balance of payments is one centred upon 'expenditure switching' and 'expenditure absorbing' policies. These are used to maintain both an internal and an external balance for the economy, as connected through relevant internal expenditure multipliers and import/export elasticities. It was these 'real' variables that concerned 'Keynesian' policy makers and formed the context in which the external balance (via exchange rate manipulation) could be maintained at the same time as an internal balance (via fiscal policy) managed - if with difficulty at times (Caves and Jones 1973, Chapter 18).

However, with the advent of floating exchange rates and the growth of new forms of international monetary instruments (like Eurocurrencies), coupled with the progressive integration of money and capital markets on a world scale, and with the development of large OPEC surplus, <u>capital movements</u> within the international economy began to dominate balance of payments and exchange rate considerations. Speculative capital movements on a very large scale began to undermine national systems designed to control capital movements, and individual governments found it increasingly difficult to resist pressures for de-control. Added to this was a growing awareness of inflation as a significant and entrenched 'problem' for individual countries which itself affected their ability to withstand speculative pressures and capital movements into and out of their currencies.

A number of these developments are considered in greater detail in the next chapter, but as far as their impact on conceptions of the balance of payments is concerned this gave rise to a change from this being fundamentally seen as determined or caused by 'real' factors to it increasingly being thought as determined or caused by 'monetary' flows and considerations. This shift of concern can also be represented with the aid of equation (1).

If we aggregate the first three items on the right hand side of this equation, these are the domestic counterparts of monetary growth and they can be termed domestic credit expansion (DCE). In addition, the EF item on the right hand side will appear as a capital item in the form of the central bank's holdings of gold and foreign exchange reserves (FA). Thus (1) can be rewritten as:

$$\triangle Ms = DCE + \triangle FA \dots\dots\dots\dots\dots (3)$$

If we now make an assumption about the relationship between money supply and money demand (M_d) such that $Ms = M_d$ (i.e. the money market clears) then (3) can be rearranged as follows:

$$\triangle FA = \triangle M_d - DCE \dots\dots\dots\dots\dots (4)$$

The equation forms the basis of the monetary approach to the balance of payments. It turns what was previously an identity into a behavioural equation which can now be used to develop an argument about the causal connections between the three items specified in equation (4): The change in foreign exchange reserves (FA), or what amounts to the same thing the balance of payments, is equal to and determined by the change in the demand for money (M_d) less the increase in domestic credit expansion (DCE). Thus the balance of payments is caused by monetary factors, in the first instance, and here lies the meaning of the 'reverse causality' argument. Instead of the real features

14

causing the monetary ones in a Keynesian fashion, it is monetary features that now cause real features of the balance of payments. It is approaches based upon this equation that have tended to dominate in the late 1970s and early 1980s. Any 'disequilibrium' between money demand and 'money supply' (DCE) will thus appear as a change in the external accounts.

3. CONTROLLING THE MONEY SUPPLY AND THE PSBR

Given the above framework the issue becomes one of working on two fronts: on the one hand directly controlling the PSBR via a more stringent control over (or even reduction in) public expenditure and, on the other hand, a control over the money supply itself to defeat inflation and in turn to put downward pressure on the PSBR.

With respect to the PSBR it is important to note that this concept is a relatively new one to economic debates. It was a term hardly heard of in the 1950s and 1960s. Only in the mid 1970s did it become significant in the context of economic policy. As Table 2.1 demonstrates this coincided with a period in which PSBR both increased as a percentage of overall government expenditure and as a percentage of GDP. The reason it became a significant 'problem' in this period was that it became a problem to finance. It appeared as a central indicator of the confidence of the private sector financial markets in the economic policies of the government of the day from about 1973/74 onwards (see Thompson 1985).

In addition if we now look at government expenditure levels as a percentage of GDP these also peaked in the mid 1970s, as Figure 2.1 shows. The picture here is one of growing trend over the twenty year period between 1963/64 and 1983/84.

In terms of the absolute levels of government expenditure this has continued to grow in real terms under the Conservatives despite a rhetoric of cutbacks and retrenchment. This is shown in Table 2.2. (See also Chart 1, HMSO (1984) p.5). When appropriate adjustments are made to the published expenditure figures as issued by the government to present them on a comparable year by year basis and to convert them into constant cost terms it can be seen that general public expenditure increased by nearly 10% over the period 1979/80 to 1983/84 (12.3% from 1978/79). It is interesting to note

Table 2.1: The PSBR as a % of Total Public Expenditure and of GDP. 1960 - 1979

Year	% of Total Public Expenditure	% of GDP
	(1)	(2)
1960	7.55	
61	6.82	
62	4.96	
63	7.22	3
64	7.75	3
65	8.52	3
66	6.27	2
67	10.63	5
68	6.69	3
69	0	-1
1970	0	0
71	5.64	2
72	7.48	3
73	12.90	6
74	15.11	8
75	19.31	10
76	16.35	7
77	9.3	4
78	12.2	5
79	16.1	6

Source: Column (1): Tomlinson (1981) Table 1 p.388; Column (2): National Income and Expenditure Blue Books (various years).

from this table that in terms of expenditure by economic category, fixed investment is the only one to show a <u>fall</u> in real expenditure while total grants and subsidies (to consumption mainly) and expenditure on current goods and services increased at an above average rate.

Figure 2.1: The Growth of Government Expenditure as a % of GDP 1963/64 - 1983/84

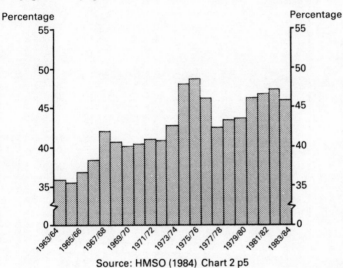

Source: HMSO (1984) Chart 2 p5

While these figures represent grossed up totals, Table 2.3 shows a more disaggregated and functional breakdown in the growth of public expenditure programmes, for the year 1983-84 compared to 1980-81. It can be seen that, again, after suitable adjustments, overall public expenditure increased by 9.2% (the final line) though within this there have been some significant variations[2]. This table can also be used to pick out one or two pertinent points that go to underline a number of current issues within popular political discussion. In the first place it can be seen that while 'Defence' and 'Law and Order' show strong real increases these are by no means the front runners on this score. Secondly the figures for net EEC payments go some way to show why Mrs Thatcher has been so adamant on the EEC budget payment issue. But reducing these

17

Table 2.2: The Growth of Public Expenditure 1978-79 to 1983-84 and Forecasts for 1984-85 to 1986-87 (All in real terms)

	1978-9	1979-80	1980-1	1981-2	1982-3	1983-4	1984-5	1985-6	1986-7
Planning Total - as published in cash terms	65,752	76,922	92,672	104,676	113,377	120,328	126,353	132,080	136,680
		£ millions at 1982-83 prices							
Planning Total - in cost terms	106,857	106,989	108,588	111,624	113,377	114,598	114,606	114,917	114,620
- in cost terms, adjusted	110,439	113,147	114,271	117,652	120,411	124,007	124,906	124,904	124,248
		Cost Terms, Index numbers, 1978-79 = 100.0							
Planning Total - as published	100.0	101.1	101.6	104.5	106.1	107.2	107.3	107.5	107.3
- adjusted	100.0	102.5	103.5	106.5	109.0	112.3	113.1	113.1	112.5
By Economic Category									
- current goods and services	100.0	105.2	108.4	113.3	115.0	118.4	118.2	118.0	117.5
- of which, salaries and wages	100.0	101.0	105.7	106.8	107.2	109.2	108.4	107.1	105.7
- fixed investment	100.0	99.1	90.9	78.5	76.2	79.7	68.7	70.2	69.6
- total grants and subsidies	100.0	100.8	101.3	106.9	113.9	117.8	114.6	115.0	114.7
By Spending Authority									
- central Government	100.0	102.7	104.5	107.9	112.1	111.2	111.8	111.6	111.1
- local authorities	100.0	102.8	100.7	97.5	100.1	106.9	99.8	98.4	96.9

Note: For the purpose of these calculations the following assumptions have been made:
(a) a GDP deflator increase of 4.25% has been assumed for 1985-86;
(b) a GDP deflator increase of 3.75% has been assumed for 1986-87;
(c) unallocated local authority expenditure is assumed to go entirely to salary and wages .

The adjusted planning totals allow for the effect of progressive changes in national insurance surcharges, the changed treatment of housing and sickness benefits, and the negative effect of special asset sales, and net debt interest. The fixed investment figures for 1984-85, 1985-86 and 1986-87 are adjusted to allow for the privatization of British Telecom, which will no longer be included as part of the public sector from 1984-85 onwards.

Source: Table 1: Treasury and Civil Service Committee 3rd Report: _The Governments Expenditure Plans 1984-85 to 1986-87._ HCP 285 March 1984.

18

payments may well simply throw a good deal of the agricultural support element back onto domestic expenditure and hence inflate the domestic agricultural budget even further. In the Appendix to this chapter the issue of the Government position on the EEC payments issue is further discussed.

Thirdly the figures for social security expenditure could help explain why the Conservatives launched an extensive review of the social services in the early part of 1984. It was stressed at the time however that this did not necessarily imply the object of such an exercise was deliberately to cut back on expenditure in this field though this looks likely to be the outcome. The complex issue of social security is discussed again in Chapters 5 and 7 below.

Finally it is interesting to note that expenditure on the Health Services <u>increased</u> over the period by 5.8% and is even planned to increase by another 2.5% in real terms to 1986-87. Whilst modest and certainly not sufficient to provide for all the urgent and necessary requirements in this field it does somewhat undermine the cry of the 'destruction of the NHS'. In Chapter 5 this issue is discussed in greater detail.

Real cutbacks have been experienced in Industry and Transport (though here this is accounted for by the relative decline in the importance of support for the Nationalized Industries in these sectors), in other Public Services and particularly in Housing. Asset sales show the most significant 'negative' effect, though these are netted out along with other adjustments to arrive at the comparable real figure of 9.2% increase in total public expenditure between 1980/81 and 1983/84.

Despite a consistent pattern of <u>planned</u> reductions in public expenditure over the life of the Conservative administrations in each year successive White Papers have shown that these planned reductions have actually resulted in real increases in outturns.[3] It is perhaps not surprising then that achieving real <u>reductions</u> in public expenditure levels has now been de-emphasised by Mrs Thatcher and Mr Nigel Lawson, the Chancellor. Both hinted in mid 1984 that this was no longer their objective. Rather the objective was to hold public expenditure to current levels so that, as GDP expanded, its percentage claim on overall resources would diminish.

Table 2.3: Growth of Public Expenditure by Programme 1980-81 to 1983-84: % Change in Real Terms.

Net Payments to the EEC	83.9	
Common Services	29.9	
Social Security	25.5	
Agriculture	23.9	
Law and Order	19.0	
Defence	14.2	
Northern Ireland	7.9	
Arts	6.0	
Health	5.8	
Overseas Aid and Services	4.4	
Scotland	3.3	(0.1)
Other Environmental Services	0.6	(1.5)
Wales	0.0	(0.1)
Education	0.0	
Industry and Energy	− 3.8	(14.0)
Transport	− 5.1	(9.8)
Other Public Services	−16.1	
Housing	−49.3	
Asset Sales	−63.5	
Planning Total	7.0	
Planning excluding asset sales	7.7	
Planning excluding asset sales and net sales of land and buildings	8.4	
Net interest	26.7	
TOTAL EXPENDITURE (including interest)	9.2	

Note: Figures in brackets give cost changes without Nationalized Industry support.

Source: Adapted from Table 7 of HCP 285 (op cit) p.26.

Moving back to the PSBR itself, the history of targeting and controlling this since 1980 has proved a chequered one. Given the difficulties in reducing expenditures at a time of recession, forecasts of the PSBR have gone very much astray at times. For instance the 1980-81 target of £8.5 billions actually resulted in an outturn figure of £13 billions. The 1982-83 PSBR of £9.2 billions was £1.7 billion greater than the Treasury estimate at the time of the March 1982 Budget. In recent years, however, the Tories have been more successful in controlling these levels. In the March 1983 Budget the target was set at £8.2 billion for 1983/84 and the outturn of £9.8 billion was reasonably close to this.

In general then the PSBR has proved more difficult to target and control than at first thought - it being the difference between two large aggregate figures all the components of which are highly sensitive to changes in underlying economic conditions. But the Government has managed to reduce it as a percentage of GDP. In 1976-77 this proportion was 6.7%, in 1981-82 it was down to 3.4% and in 1983-84 the target of 2.75% was slightly overshot to emerge as an actual figure of 3.25% of GDP. The consequences of this declining proportion are examined further in the next section. Thus while the absolute level of the PSBR has proved difficult to forecast and control closely, the money figure of some £8-£9 billions at the end of 1983 - the same in nominal terms as at the end of 1974 - represents a deflated value of about half this magnitude. By any account the PSBR in 1983 was a much smaller 'burden' than when the Conservatives gained office.

Turning now to the growth of the money supply proper, one of the early problems, before attempts at controlling it could be organized, was to find a reasonable measure of the money supply. A measure termed Sterling M3 seemed to be appropriate[4]. It provided a convenient and well understood indicator within the financial system. Indeed targets with respect to this had been introduced well before the Conservatives took office, as Table 2.4 demonstrates. The target bands for £M3 over the period from 1977 to 1984 are reproduced here and compared to their outturn. It is clear from a look at the final column that overshooting of the target has been endemic during the period of the Conservative administrations. The overshooting is further disguised in the table by the procedure of revising targets each year (and sometimes at intervals of less than a year). Most of the original target periods were set for fourteen to eighteen months but these were then (and still are) revised at the time of successive Budget statements. It is sometimes claimed that this yearly change in the targets demonstrates the close reactive character of the authorities in their determination to

21

control the money supply. But it could also be considered a weakness in that they are 'reacting' here rather than 'directing' in their efforts. All the actual growth rates have been near the top of or above the range set except for the year 83-84, when the outturn was well within the range set by the target.

Table 2.4: Target Growth of £M3 and Actual Outturns (1976-1984)

Date Announced	Period	Target Range %	Outturn %	Error(a) %	
Dec 1976	Apr 76-Apr 77	9 - 13	7.7	- 1.3	
Mar 1977	Apr 77-Apr 78	9 - 13	16.0	+ 3.0	
Apr 1978	Apr 78-Apr 79	8 - 12	10.9	-	
Nov 1978	Oct 78-Oct 79	8 - 12	13.3	+ 1.3	
Jun 1979	Jun 79-Apr 80	7 - 11	10.3	-	Change in
Nov 1979	Jun 79-Oct 80	7 - 11	17.8	+ 6.8	Government
Mar 1980	Feb 80-Apr 81	7 - 11	22.2	+11.2	
Mar 1981	Feb 81-Apr 82	6 - 10	13.5	+ 3.5	
Mar 1982	Apr 82-Apr 83	8 - 12	12.25	-	
Mar 1983	Feb 83-Apr 84	7 - 11	9.9	-	
Mar 1984	Feb 84-Apr 85	5 - 9	11.6	+ 2.6	

Note: (a) Difference between the outturn and top or bottom of target range.

Source: NIER Nov 1982 p.40 Table 1, plus author's own updating

4.   THE MTFS: AN ASSESSMENT

Assessments of the MTFS have differed largely according to the theoretical stance adopted by commentators. 'Monetarists' broadly speaking, have been sympathetic to its intentions and pronounced it a measured success (eg Budd 1983 and 1984). 'Keynesians', on the other hand have taken up a more critical stance and distanced themselves from the manner with which macro-economic policy has been approached, if not altogether with the intentions of this policy (eg. Buiter and Miller 1981 and 1983). Those further to the left of the political spectrum either view it as a disaster for the economy in terms of its unemployment and output consequences (eg Coutts et al 1981) or, in a wider context, see it as a response to the declining rate of accumulation of capital and an attempt to transform the balance of class forces within the economy overall (eg Cowling 1984).

Whilst not unsympathetic to these latter positions the assessment conducted here will initially concentrate upon the more Keynesian critique and then develop some critical remarks with respect to this position. Such an approach is in line with the attempt to develop an assessment of the MTFS and of the Conservatives' strategy more generally, largely from within its own terms, rather than from positions that begin from a totally different and often competing theoretical perspective.

The context for the more Keynesian position can be discussed by reference to the data plotted in Figure 2.2. This shows two measures of the public sector's nominal need to borrow and 'fiscal stance' - the PSBR itself and the public sector financial deficit (PSFD - this is also sometimes referred to as public sector 'fiscal' deficit) over the period 1967 to 1982 (definitions of these and the other measures are given in the notes to this figure). The growth in the nominal value of the PSBR is shown here. The so called 'crisis' of public expenditure in 1974-75 can be clearly seen from the figure. This was the period in which the PSBR escalated and for a while became the main 'problem' for the economy. To a large extent it was this episode that propelled the levels of public spending and the PSBR into a prominence that still lingers with respect to macro-economic management.

However two other measures are also plotted in Figure 2.2. These 'adjust' the PSFD for the effects of inflation. The point here is that during times of rapid inflation debtors gain at the expense of creditors. This is because the nominal value of debt declines in real terms. Debts are normally contracted in money terms and with inflation in money values the obligation of the debt in terms of current money values declines. The State, as a net debtor, thus 'gains' during periods of accelerating inflation. Its debt burden declines in real terms. To specify financing obligations in nominal money terms is thus misleading it is suggested. This has led a number of economists to argue for various forms of adjustment to be made with respect to government debt and the borrowing requirement,

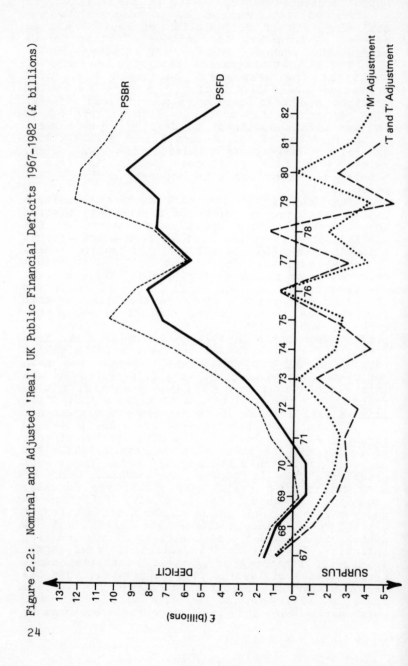

Figure 2.2: Nominal and Adjusted 'Real' UK Public Financial Deficits 1967–1982 (£ billions)

The 'Medium Term Financial Strategy'

Sources and Definitions for Graph

Definitions

PSBR	=	Nominal Public Sector Borrowing Requirement
PSFD	=	Nominal Public Sector Financial Deficit (defined as Public Sector expenditure minus tax receipts plus the interest (gross of tax) paid on the stock of Treasury Bills, ie the nominal value of the Public Sector Debt)
'T and T' Adjustment	=	Inflation adjusted 'real' PSFD on the basis of Taylor and Threadgold (1979) calculations, as reported in Miller (1982)
'M' Adjustment	=	Inflation adjusted 'real' PSFD on the basis of Miller (1982) and Miller and Babbs (1983) calculations

Note: 1982 values are approximate in this diagram.

notable amongst these have been Marcus Miller (1982) and Willem Buiter (1983). To some extent this position has been endorsed by the Bank of England itself. It was two of the Bank's economists who first provided the rationale for this kind of adjustment (Taylor and Threadgold 1979) and the Bank has subsequently continued publishing an annual update of their figures (to be found in Bank of England Quarterly Bulletin, June of each year).

In Figure 2.2 the PSFD has been adjusted on the basis of Taylor and Threadgold's figures ('T and T' Adjustment) and on the basis of Miller's figures ('M' Adjustment). Both of these show a rather similar trend. The important point here is that in 'real' terms the government sector has been in more or less continual surplus over the whole period specified. A nominal deficit is transformed into a 'real' surplus (or at minimum a real 'balance budget' position). The argument is that this demonstrates rather more of a continuity than is often recognised between the Conservative Government's stance on government budgeting and that of its predecessors. It is well known that the government's budgetary stance throughout the 1950s and 60s was rather more deflationary than it was inflationary (Mathews 1968, Tomlinson 1981) and this position, in 'real' terms, has continued into the 1970s and early 1980s.

Indeed it could be argued that given the deep recession that ensued during the 1970s and 1980s the basic 'surplus' position on the budgetary account encouraged and deepened this recession in the UK. Whilst it might look as though the government ran up a 'Keynesian' budget deficit during this recession (albeit reluctantly), in fact it pursued a stong deflationary policy in a rather conventional and orthodox manner. Given the relative failure of money supply control mechanisms as pointed out in the context of Table 2.4, monetary policy has been more 'lax' than it might otherwise have been. The implication of this argument is that far from 'monetarism' sweeping away fiscal and budgetary policy, it has been the basic budgetary position of the government that has 'sustained' the recession and brought about the disinflation that the government required.[5] Indeed this was something that was developing well before the Conservatives took office. Their 'monetarism' had only a marginal impact on this. Clearly if an economy is deflated hard enough and over a sustained enough period of time prices are bound to fall eventually. The fact that price rises are now in single figures is largely a result of this mechanism along with its attendant side-effects, growing unemployment and declining production.

Interestingly enough it was not Buiter and Miller themselves who explicitly made this crucial point but, as footnote 5 makes clear, it was left to one of their commentators to state it explicitly. Admittedly also, the PSFD went into 'surplus' in year 1983 since the 'real' PSBR became negative (-£5.8 billion) in that year and the 'real' PSFD stood at £4.9 billions. (BEQB June 1984 Table C p.233). This is mainly because of the reduction in inflation, but achieved, it might be added, as a result of the positive 'real' position for the years proceeding this.

The difficulty over pursuing a 'monetarist' monetary policy is exemplified by the way in which the Bank of England has continued to intervene significantly in the private money markets and on the international exchanges in an attempt to gain control over its money supply targets and influence interest rates. In fact to a large extent it has increased its levels of intervention on this score (rather than withdrawing from intervention as rhetoric would have it) - defining and targeting a new and increasing range of policy variables. In the March 1982 Budget for instance three monetary targets were specified rather than the single £M3. This was supplemented with a narrower measure of monetary growth M1 and a wider measure PSL_2 [6] - all targeted in a range of 7 - 11% for 1983-4. During that year actual growth of these was 11.1% and 12.3% respectively, both outside of the target range. Again this should seriously question the relevance of these as monetary target variables and the viability of the policy more generally.

The problem here is that the three aggregates are not likely to increase in line for a number of reasons. For instance interest rates affect M1 and £M3 quite differently. Increasing interests rates encourage people to put their money on deposit (so that it earns a rate of return). This reduces M1 relative to £M3 since people will move out of holding current accounts and notes and coin, which do not realise a return. As interest rates fall, the convenience of a large current account balance costs less in terms of these foregone interest payments, so M1 grows faster than £M3 as people switch back. In addition financial innovation, particularly by the Building Societies is driving a wedge between £M3 and PSL_2. This latter includes Building Society Deposits whereas £M3 does not. As the Societies progressively turn themselves into conventional banks with chequing account facilities, and compete for funds with variable interest rate policies, they attract assets out of £M3 (the Commercial Banks) and into PSL_2. In addition for all practical intents and purposes all Building Society accounts can be viewed as demand accounts, PSL_2 excludes some of the longer term Building Society accounts but these can be quite easily converted into demand deposits, thus 'artifically' increasing PSL_2 under varying conditions. All this just goes to make clear how difficult it is to control the money supply in a developed financial system.[7] The Conservatives have been no more successful at this than would be governments of a different political persuasion.

Indeed, largely because of the problems

mentioned immediately above a _further_ money supply measure was added for targeting in the March 1984 budget. A very narrow measure M_0 - or notes and coin only - was introduced mainly as a result of a disenchantment with the performance of M1. M_0 is close to the so called 'high-powered' money that some technical monetarists would like to see used in connection with a base control mechanism of monetary control. The general idea here is that if this 'base' of the banks credit multiplier can be controlled so can the credit or money that the commercial banks generate within the system. In particular a reduction in the amount of this base money will lead to a multiple reduction in the credit money circulating within the economy. Given a connection between such money circulation and price formation, inflation can also be indirectly controlled. [8]

There are a number of problems with this position, most of which have been elaborated by the Bank of England itself. In the first place it still harks back to a conception of money supply creation based directly upon textbook 'credit multiplier' analysis and banks reserve ratios. However, as long ago as 1963 James Tobin pointed out that this conception was inadequate (Tobin 1963). He suggested banks should be analysed, like any other commercial organization, in terms of profit maximization and the relationship between the marginal cost of deposits and the marginal yield on loans. [9] Developing this line of analysis has led economists like Goodhart (1984 p.16) to stress the way banks and other financial institutions will try to circumvent any controls put on them in order to maximize their profits. In addition in 1980 the Bank of England abandoned the use of reserve ratio as a mechanism for trying to control the Commercial Banks credit creation activities, so altering the framework of regulation. Money supply growth must now be situated in this more complex context where the rather simple 'base-credit multiplier' analysis becomes inadequate.

Secondly, and connected to this, there is a problem for the authorities in engineering a shortage in any such 'base money', given the rapidly innovating and flexible financial systems that typify modern developed economies. A whole range of new 'cash' producing mechanisms are in the process of being developed, not simply within the banking system narrowly defined (eg by Building Societies and Retail Shops). This renders generating a realistic scarcity in such base money extremely difficult if not impossible. This is just another way of pointing to the instability and volatile nature of any 'demand function' for base-money (Johnston 1984).

As mentioned above these difficulties have long been recognised by the Bank of England. The Bank has stuck to using the broad money supply aggregate £M3 as its main target variable despite efforts to promote a much narrower focus, initially on M1 and then on M_0 as the appropriate central measure. This is not simply a technical definitional problem however since going over to a more monetarist 'base control' method akin to M_0 would have meant that short-term interest rates would have been more or less the only feasible instrument to use for control. This could produce even more volatile movements in such rates, with a consequent severe disruption of the financial sector and of the real sector of the economy as well. These the Bank wanted to protect and supervise. The long term consequence of such a monetarist move would also have been a significant reduction in the ability of the Bank to undertake what it saw as a proper supervision and regulation of the financial system. To allow absolutely 'free' market mechanisms to set interest rates and determine the amount of money in the economy, which was the position being advocated by some of the monetarists advising the Treasury, was resisted by the Bank. The Bank still wanted to maintain a firmer leaverage over various monetary instruments and over the financial system in general despite the abandonment of exchange controls in the autumn of 1979 and all remaining direct controls on the money supply in the summer of 1980. In effect it rejected the advice implied by the radical 'monetarist' critics of its position (eg Griffiths et al in HMSO 1980) and this has been very well recognized by those critics (eg Batchelor 1983).[10] Thus to some extent the Bank of England operated as a constant critic of the monetary policy being thrust upon it from the Government and the Treasury in the period from 1980. There were thus some important differences amongst the state apparatuses about how to conduct economic management during the early 1980s. Some of this is more or less admitted in a very frank and widely quoted discussion of the monetary policy of the period that appeared in the Bank of England Quarterly Bulletin (Fforde 1983). In this Fforde de-emphasises the role of economic doctrine in determining the

29

actual policy pursued, but emphasises what he terms the 'political economy' of target setting. In summing up the experience of UK monetary targeting he suggests:

> ....that it would scarcely have been possible to mount and carry through, over several years and without resort to direct controls of all kinds, so determined a counter inflationary strategy if it had not been for the initial 'political economy' of the firm monetary target. Though not considered at the time, it would have been possible to initiate such a strategy with a familiar 'Keynesian' exposition about managing demand downwards, and with greater concentration on ultimate objectives than on intermediate targets. But this would have meant disclosing objectives for, inter alia, output and employment. This would have been a very hazardous exercise, and the objectives would either have been unacceptable to public opinion or else inadequate to secure a substantial reduction in the rate of inflation, or both. Use of strong intermediate targets, for money supply and government borrowing, enabled the authorities to stand back from output and employment as such and to stress the vital part to be played in respect of these by the trend of industrial costs. In short, whatever the subsequent difficulties of working with intermediate targets, they were vitally important at the outset in order to signal a decisive break with the past and enable the authorities to set out with presentational confidence upon a relatively uncharted sea.
> (Fforde 1983 p.207).

Monetary targets were thus a rather convenient, pragmatic and largely 'presentational' device behind which to conduct a 'familiar Keynesian' deflation of the economy, without the inconvenience of having to specify the likely real output and employment consequences. This reinforces the arguments made above about the character and implications of the 'real budgetary' position of the economy. A rather orthodox deflation was the order of the day.

Of course we must not press this argument further than is justified. It is not to suggest that the level of the nominal PSBR was unproblematical for the authorities. Whether the 'real' budget was in surplus, balanced, or in deficit even, would have made little difference to the necessity and problem associated with financing the nominal deficit. This did prove problematical, given the reluctance of the financial system to hold a quick increase in such debt. Debt management took on a renewed importance during this period, as is exemplified by the rise in interest rates in the mid to late 1970s and the continual struggle to influence these since. In fact it was just this interest rate manipulation that became the main policy instrument deployed to try and control money supply growth during this period. Such interest rate manipulation is condemned by 'monetarists' as it is thought to be a 'Keynesian' monetary mechanism that operates through influencing the <u>demand</u> for money in the first instance, rather than its supply.

Nor is this to argue that the government was unconstrained on the monetary or budetary front during this period. Clearly it could hardly have 'reflated' out of the recession in isolation from other countries by, say, cutting taxes dramatically or borrowing and spending more. If nothing else the international position precluded this kind of response - something taken up in greater detail in the next chapter. Finally we must not overemphasise either the 'Keynesianism' or the 'monetarism' of what actually took place. The worldwide recession - caused by a diverse range of circumstances - was on its way and largely dictated events in the UK. In the face of this there was (and is) little room for manoeuvre by governments whether Keynesian or monetarist in outlook. Clearly there was a switch of emphasis here - away from targeting 'real' variables and into targeting 'monetary' ones, but perhaps even Fforde over-emphasises the actual role played by monetary targeting when judged against the relative failure of this as a technique. If we restrict 'monetarism' to the narrow focus of simply attempting to regulate an economy via controlling the money supply - its central premiss - then the UK demonstrates its 'failure' in this period. What effective policy there was only went to deepen a recession, itself produced by forces largely outside of government control and rather independent of either Keynesianism or monetarism.

A further point is worth raising in this discussion of the relative effectiveness or

31

otherwise of the MTFS. One of the 'successes' claimed for it is the progressive reduction in the PSBR/GDP ratio, as referred to above on page 21. This is now at an historically low level, (as is the total nominal outstanding debt to GDP ratio). The question this raises is what is happening to the financial flows in the economy if these are not now being channeled into government debt? The idea here was to squeeze the public sector borrowing as a proportion of GDP so as to release funds for private investment and use - the so called 'crowding in' effect. But there is little sign that such private sector investment opportunities are arising - at least not in the domestic economy. While there has been some revival in the fortunes of the Stock Exchange's private issue business (discussed more fully in Chapter 3), most of the now available funds seem to be going abroad. As mentioned above exchange controls were abandoned in the autumn of 1979. Largely as a result, gross UK portfolio investment overseas has risen rapidly since then. This is attributed to buoyant security prices (particularly in the USA) and to the depreciation of sterling since 1980 (which added some £7.4 billion to the value of this investment in 1982). But new net purchases are also significant at nearly £6 billion in 1982 of which approximately £4 billions was generated by the financial institutions outside of the banking sector. Very similar levels to these have been reported for 1983 (BEQR June 1984 p.226). All in all UK private sector assets held abroad have doubled in value between 1980 and 1983 to $US 110 billions with a huge net value of $US 81 billions. Thus the absence of internally generated assets into which the financial institutions might channel their monetary flows, has resulted in these being invested abroad. Interestingly enough the market in US Treasury Bonds and Notes has been buoyant. In 1983 the US was running a Federal deficit of some $200 billions and a deficit to GNP ratio of 6.5%, roughly twice the UK figure.[11]

Table 2.5 shows the overseas holdings of US Treasury Bonds and Notes for a selected group of European and other countries. Germany and the UK in Europe demonstrate the largest increases between 1982 and 1983.

Thus what has been happening is that the UK financial institutions are helping to finance a US budget deficit. This might seem a rather bizarre result in the context of the UK economy. Britain is

Table 2.5: Overseas Holdings of Marketable US Treasury Bonds and Notes: Selected Countries ($ millions)

	1982	%	1983	%
Estimated Total	85,169		88,990	
Europe	29,274	34.4	35,482	39.9
Belguim and Luxembourg	447	0.5	16	0.0
Germany	14,841	17.4	17,290	19.4
Netherlands	2,754	3.2	3,129	3.5
Sweden	667	0.8	842	0.9
Switzerland	1,540	1.8	1,118	1.3
UK	6,549	7.7	8,524	9.6
Other W Europe	2,469	2.9	4,563	5.1
Canada	602	0.7	1,301	1.5
Japan	11,578	13.6	13,910	15.6

Note: Excludes non-marketable US Treasury Bonds and Notes held by official institutions of foreign countries.

Source: Federal Reserve Bulletin, April 1984, Table A6-3.

helping directly to reflate the US economy!
This makes the claim that there is no room for any domestic reflationary government borrowing ring rather hollow. Clearly there seems to be at least some room for manoeuvre here. Indeed this has been recognized by both the TUC and the CBI who have called for an increase in government funded capital investment expenditure financed by borrowing (see Glyn 1983).

For the Government however the reduction and control of inflation has been and continues to be its primary and dominant economic objective.[12] It has held to this with great tenacity and obstinacy in the face of a changing set of economic conditions. But it has also been flexible in terms of how this objective might be achieved. When the early drastic attack on the levels of public sector expenditure seemed to be faltering it switched the emphasis to trying to control the money supply directly. As we have seen, this was not at all successful and subsequently the government began to take more notice of the exchange rate and its consequences for inflation and the domestic economy. More recently, along with this, the role of public spending has again come to the fore. All this suggests that the Conservatives have been quite flexible in the face of the constraints that they have encountered in their attempts to reduce inflation.

5. CONCLUSIONS

Has the MTFS been a success? Clearly the answer to this question partly depends upon one's political and economic priorities. Inflation has been reduced to single figures but at an enormous 'cost' in terms of unemployment and loss of output. Figure 2.3 shows what has happened to manufacturing production during the period of the Tories being in office. The dramatic fall between 1979 and 1981 has yet to be recouped, but a recovery of sorts seems to be underway as of 1983. It also depends upon whether one feels a viable alternative was possible which could have avoided the unemployment and output losses without at the same time offsetting these with increasingly unstable inflationary conditions.

The burden of this chapter, however, has been to look at the MTFS from a slightly different angle - to judge it more in terms of whether it has met its pretentions. In so doing we have also been able to interrogate some of the problems with the implementation of a seemingly monetarist strategy. The argument has been that on both these counts the strategy has been found wanting. By and large the MTFS turned into an orthodox deflation largely because of the difficulties of controlling economies via simple monetary rules and procedures. This also helps highlight a further point of contrast with more orthodox accounts of this episode in economic management. The argument here is that it is unhelpful to consider the Conservatives' approach as heralding a radical displacement of one prevailing theoretical orthodoxy - 'Keynesianism' - by another - termed 'monetarism'. Theoretical differences are important but policy implementation does not follow unproblematically from these differences. Indeed, if one pays less attention to theoretical differences a fuller understanding of the constraints on economic policy making emerge and in so doing the continuities in such policy appear more obviously. This theme will be continued in subsequent chapters of this book.

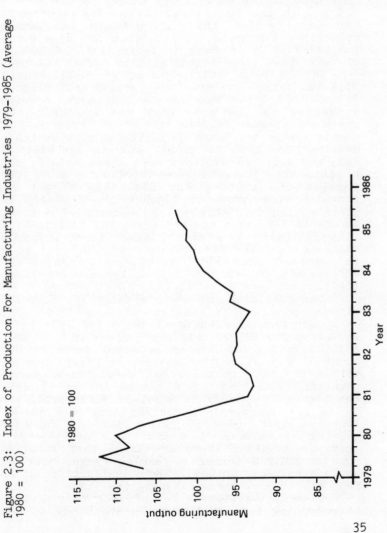

Figure 2.3: Index of Production For Manufacturing Industries 1979-1985 (Average 1980 = 100)

Appendix : The UK and the EEC Budget Problem

Since Britain joined the EEC in 1973 there seems to have been a more or less continuous guerrilla warfare going on between Britain and the other members, none more so virulently than during the period of Mrs Thatcher's administration. That the UK has had a ambivalent attitude towards the EEC goes virtually without saying. The issue that came to a head in the early 1980s concerned the growing EEC budget and the 'inequitable' distribution of the finance for this as between the member countries. The gross contributions of these during the early 1980s is shown in Table A1.1. In 1984 the UK was the largest contributor after Germany. Of the total EEC budget of £14.5 billions in 1984 two thirds was spent on agricultural support. It was this issue that became the major 'problem' appearing on the political agenda during the somewhat fierce negotiations that occupied EEC Commissioners and Heads of State during a series of meetings designed to hammer out an agreement in 1983 and early 1984. There were three main aspects of these negotiations. One involved a short term problem of limiting an escalating budget and providing the means to finance it. Secondly and closely tied into this was a question of a rebate to the UK for its inequitable general contribution. Finally there was the longer term issue of restructuring EEC finances and expenditures so as to 'solve' Britain's particular problem and effectively reform the Common Agriculture Policy (CAP).

CAP subsidies and their effects are notorious within popular discussion of the EEC. Milk overproduction is running at 14.5% for 1984 (which will cost the EEC £2 billions). Since 1977 of the 2 million tonnes of butter produced annually only about 1.5 million tonnes is actually consumed within the EEC, so there has developed a 'butter mountain' absorbing 3.5 m tonnes (a lot of which has been sold cheaply to Russia). Wheat production is in chronic surplus, ranging from 4 m to 6 m tonnes a year. The EEC 'wine lake' is currently growing by between 15 m and 20 m hectolitres a year. In addition there are large beef surpluses (up to 300,000 tonnes a year), orange, pear and apple surpluses. Cotton, sugar, sunflower seeds and rape oil are new items entering the list.

Clearly there are a set of long term problems here begging serious discussion about how to deal with them. Mrs Thatcher has chosen to take an 'adversary' stance on this, arguing on a seemingly selfish platform of 'what's good for Britain is going to be good for the Community overall'. The net position with respect to the UK's particular contribution and receipt profile is shown in Table A1.2.

It has been the growing net contribution of the UK, shown in the final line of the Table A1.2, that has galvanized the Conservatives into action. Given that the relative position of the UK economy has been declining in the European context it has been generally agreed that the UK's long term contribution should be cut and indeed that rebates on the early 1980s position installed. The 1984 figures shown in the Table represent planned figures. These became quickly out of date during 1984 as the EEC budget escalated to a predicted £1.4 bn deficit.

The framework for an agreement hammered out in the spring of 1984 at the Fontainebleau summit involved putting a VAT ceiling on EEC finances of 1.4% and organizing a rebate for the UK to cut its estimated net contribution in 1984 by half. This latter feature was blocked by the EEC Parliament and at the time of writing is still unsettled. The settlement of the longer term problems was essentially put-off until the EEC's budget income was exhausted within the agreed 1.4% VAT ceiling. In the meantime the Commission would present its own solution to these problems so that the series of adhoc and temporary arrangements involving the UK's payments could be finally settled towards the end of 1984/beginning of 1985. CAP reform would be central here as at present any increase in spending on farm support has a disproportionate effect on UK payments. A probable compromise will be simply to express additional payments as a percentage of GNP - at least as an interim measure.

The question all this raises is whether the framework for the agreement worked out as above represented quite such a 'triumph' for Mrs Thatcher and for Britain as was made out. Any answer to this cannot be divorced from the wider issue of what is thought to be the correct role for the UK to play within Europe. At present the UK's position is both strong and weak. It is strong in the sense that its net contribution to the budget is significant and the withdrawal of the UK would present very difficult financial adjustments for the other members. On the other hand its position is weak in that it has played a very negative role within the Community so far, fighting for its national interests only on a very limited and selfish basis. The UK for instance has developed very few <u>positive</u> policies towards the EEC. It is hostile to full participation in the EMS and any thought of a wider monetary union. It has not pushed for policies with respect to energy or regional and social funding, where the UK would have an advantage as far as potential benefits were concerned. The Italians for instance were in a somewhat similar position as the UK when they joined the EEC, particularly over their monetary and budget difficulties, but they campaigned internally, quietly and effectively for policies that not only suited themselves but also gained wider Community support. Perhaps the time has come for a 'confrontation' type approach so beloved of Mrs Thatcher to be displaced by this kind of more positive attitude before the other Community members decide that the cost of British membership is just not worth the effort involved with its continuation.

Table A1.1: Gross Contributions to EEC Budget by Member States (£m)

	1981	1982	1983	1984
Belgium	547.3	643.2	714.0	773.9
Denmark	195.8	225.4	281.6	293.5
Germany	2794.6	3192.3	3874.9	4003.6
Greece	140.6	213.8	231.5	275.7
France	1929.3	2367.3	2678.2	2912.6
Ireland	87.8	116.8	156.1	145.0
Italy	1395.9	1393.3	1798.3	2058.2
Luxembourg	15.1	16.9	25.8	23.5
Netherlands	711.2	821.4	939.8	984.5
UK	2173.9	2862.7	2975.7	3081.0
TOTAL	9991.5	11853.1	13675.9	14551.5

Source: <u>Statement on the 1984 Community Budget</u> HMSO March 1984. Cmnd 9174, Table III A.

The 'Medium Term Financial Strategy'

Table A1.2: UK's Contributions and Receipts From the
Community Budget (£m)

	1981	1982	1983	1984
Gross Contributions				
Ag. and sugar levies	218.2	307.3	231.7	284.2
Custom duties	806.5	1001.0	1075.1	1109.8
VAT on resources	1095.2	1554.4	1668.9	1687.0
TOTAL	2119.9	2862.7	2975.7	3081.0
Receipts				
Own resources refund	113.5	133.7	129.5	139.3
EMS interest rate subsidies compensation	21.2	32.5	21.5	-
UK refunds	693.0	1109.4	807.2	572.8
Other receipts	948.8	1071.9	1332.2	1650.3
TOTAL	1776.5	2347.5	2290.4	2362.4
Net Contributions	343.4	515.2	685.3	718.6

Source: HMSO (1984) op cit Table II

The 'Medium Term Financial Strategy'

Notes

1. The PSBR comprises the difference between total public revenues from taxation and from the sale of goods and services, and total public expenditures.

2. The position of the various programmes in this table will clearly differ depending upon the base year chosen. In the Government's own Green Paper on public expenditure (HMSO 1984) a similar table is constructed but showing changes as between 1978/79 and 1983/84 (Chart 4). As a result a number of differences emerge, perhaps the most important of which is that net contributions to the EEC moves from a + 83.9% in Table 2.3 to a - 61% in the Green Paper. While there are also some other changes, broadly speaking a similar picture emerges as between changes on the different base years.

3. See Table 4, Appendix 1 of HCP 285 (1984) op cit p.23 for a detailed analysis of this.

4. Sterling M3 is defined as notes and coin in circulation with the public plus all sterling deposits (including certificates of deposit) held by UK residents, in both the public and private sectors, with the monetary sector.

5. A commentator on the Buiter and Miller (1983) paper draws out this point Most interesting is the suggestion that, perhaps unintentionally, the Thatcher government achieved a deep recession and disinflation by application of the standard Keynesian fiscal policy. The government thought that to control money growth the public sector borrowing requirement had to be reduced, so the budget was tightened. This fiscal squeeze produced a recession, but no control over money growth. (W.H. Branson in Bookings Papers on Economic Activity 1983: 2 p.372)

6. M1 equals notes and coin in circulation with the public plus sterling sight deposits held by the UK private sector with the monetary sector.
PSL2 (Private Sector Lending) is defined as the private sector components of £M3 excluding deposits with an original maturity of more than 2 years plus specified money market instruments, certificates of tax deposit, most building society shares and deposits with the NSB and National Savings instruments.

7. For a very clear account of these and other difficulties with controlling the money supply discussed below in the text, see Goodhart (1984).Goodhart is the Bank of England's Specialist

Economic Adviser on monetary matters, and in this book he demonstrates a very sceptical attitude towards money supply control.

8. Such a position is of course very controversial. The main protagonist for a connection between UK money supply growth and inflation have been Freidman and Schwartz (1982). But their position has been seriously challenged in terms of its econometric methodology by Hendry and Ericsson (1983). See also the symposium of reviews of Freidman and Schwartz's book in the Journal of Economic Literature December 1982. For the purpose of this book I do not conduct a discussion of this debate but take the position as read so that its consequences on policy initiatives and their problems can be focused on.

9. Clearly these two positions are not incompatible though they do tend to emphasize different aspects of banks' behaviour in connection to money supply creation and thus tend to produce different policy conclusions.

10. See also the debate between Alan Walters (Mrs Thatcher's Chief Economic Adviser) and Michael Parkin in Carnegie-Rochester Series on Public Policy, No.21 (1984) pp.259-294.

11. Some commentators have challenged the level of this US Federal deficit to GNP ratio (eg A.H. Meltzer and Samuel Brittan in various reports in the Financial Times) arguing that the real 'structural deficit' is only half of the nominal one. 'Cyclical' accommodation accounts for the other 50%. In their eyes this makes the US deficit less of a 'problem' from the point of view of economic management.

12. Although inflation this year has been lower than at any time in the past fifteen years, there can be no relaxation of the pressure to keep it moving down. Only two decades or so ago an inflation of 5% would have been considered too high. The government's ultimate objective is price stability.... (Nigel Lawson, Chancellor of the Exchequer. Speech at Lord Mayor's Banquet at the Mansion House on 20th October 1983).

References

Batchelor, R.A. (1983) 'British Economic Policy Under Margaret Thatcher: A Mid Term Examination' in K. Brunner and A.M. Meltzer (eds) - Money, Monetary Policy and Financial Institutions. Carnegie - Rochester Conference Series on Public Policy, vol 18, 1983, North Holland, Amsterdam.

Budd, A.P. (1983) 'The Budget of 1983' in J. Kay (ed) The Economy and the 1983 Budget Institute of Fiscal Studies London pp.65-74.

Budd, A.P. (1984) 'Macroeconomic Aspects of the 1984 Budget' in M. Keen (ed) The Economy and the 1984 Budget. Basil Blackwell Oxford. pp.8-16.

Buiter, W.H. and M.H. Miller (1981) 'The Thatcher Experiment: The First Two Years' Brookings Papers on Economic Activity 1981: 2 pp.315-367.

Buiter, W.H. (1983) 'Measurement of the Public Sector Debt and its Implication for Policy Evaluation and Design' IMF Staff Papers, Vol 30 No.2 June pp.306-346.

Buiter, W.H. and Miller, M.H. (1983) 'Changing the Rules: Economic Consequences of the Thatcher Regime' Brookings Papers on Economic Activity 1983: 2 pp.305-379.

Carnegie-Rochester Series on Public Policy No.2 (1984) 'The United Kingdom: Political Economy and Macroeconomics' A.A. Walters (pp.259-279), and 'A Comment on Walters Paper' M. Parkin (pp.281-294). North Holland, Amsterdam.

Caves, R.E. and Jones, R.W. (1973) World Trade and Payments Little, Brown and Co. Boston.

Coutts, K. et al (1981) 'The Economic Consequences of Mrs Thatcher' Cambridge Journal of Economics Vol 5 p.81-93.

Cowling, K. (1984) 'Responses to Unemployment': An Alternative Economic Strategy' in Out of Work: Perspective of Mass Unemployment Department of Economics, University of Warwick.

Fforde, J.S. (1983) 'Setting Monetary Objectives' BEQB Vol 23, No.2 June pp.200-208.

Freidman, M. and Schwartz, A.J. (1982) Monetary Trends in the United States and the United Kingdom. University of Chicago Press. Chicago, Illinois.

Glynn, D. (1983) 'Is Government Borrowing now too low?' Lloyds Bank Review No.147 January pp.21-41.

Goodhart, C.A.E. (1984): Monetary Theory and Practice: The UK Experience. MacMillan, London.

Hendry, D.F. and Ericcson, N.R. (1983) 'Assertion without Empirical Basis: An Econometric appraisal of Freidman and Schwartz' "Monetary trends in...the United Kingdom". Bank of England Panel Paper No. 22 pp.45-101.

HMSO (1980) Memoranda on Monetary Policy Treasury and Civil Service Committee, HCP 729, July, London.

HMSO (1984) Public Expenditure and Taxation in the 1990's Cmnd 9189 HMSO, London.

Johnston, R.B. (1984) 'The Demand for Non Interest Bearing Money in the United Kingdom' Treasury Working Paper No.28 February.

Mathewes, R.C.O. (1968) 'Why has Britain had Full Employment Since the War' Economic Journal Vol LXXVIII September pp.555-569.

Miller, M.H. (1982) 'Inflation - adjusting the Public Sector Financial Deficit' in The 1982 Budget (ed) J. Kay, Institute of Fiscal Studies and Basil Blackwell, Oxford.

Miller, M.H. and Babbs, S. (1983) 'The True Cost of Debt Service and the Public Sector Financial Deficit' Paper given at AUTE Conference April 1983, Oxford University.

Taylor, C. and Threadgold, A. (1979) Real National Savings and its Sectoral Composition, Bank of England Discussion Paper No.6 London, Bank of England.

Thompson, G.F. (1985) 'Objectives and Instruments' Unit 25 D210 Introduction to Economics, The Open University Press.

Tobin, J. (1963) 'Commercial Banks as Creators of "Money"' in D. Carson (ed) Banking and Monetary Studies, Homewood, Ill.

Tomlinson, J. (1981) 'The "Economic of Politics" and Public Expenditure: A Critique'. Economy and Society Vol 10 No.4 p.381-402.

Chapter 3

THE EXCHANGE RATE, MARKETS AND UNCERTAINTY

1.   INTRODUCTION

This chapter develops some of the background to the
Conservatives' economic policy making by looking at
changes wrought in the external conditions of the
UK economy over the period of the 1970s and early
1980s. It does not provide a comprehensive and
detailed statistical picture of the relative
decline of the economy in terms of various real and
monetary features - this has been dealt with
adequately elsewhere on numerous occasions (e.g.
Williams et al 1983 and Smith 1984) and by now is
well known. Rather it concentrates upon the
changing international and institutional framework
in which the British economy was set. This the
Conservatives largely 'inherited' when they came
into office in 1979 and it provides a set of
important conditions that helps explain the rise of
both 'monetarism' as an economic ideology and some
of the more detailed theoretical arguments and
policy initiatives that they subsequently inaugurated.
In particular the exchange rate and the international
position of the economy more generally are focused
upon and the question of the role of 'markets' in a
rather wider context is looked at. The chapter also
provides an opportunity to make some general
theoretical and methodological points associated
with these issues. Thus a good deal of what is
commented on below is not directly related to the
actual economic policy pursued by the Conservatives.
Rather it provides a contextualizing framework in
which their detailed policy initiative emerged. But
it is important to highlight this context. It makes
clear the way in which the Conservatives were
constrained with respect to what they could do in
terms of domestic economic policy matters. But it

also stresses the material and theoretical tendencies underway at the time. Because of these constraints and tendencies a lot of the subsequent developments outlined below would have probably taken place independently of which government was in office in the UK. Thus not everything should be attributed to the conscious policy of the particular government in power.

2.   THE EXCHANGE RATE AND FUTURE MARKETS

As was mentioned in the previous chapter, in connection with the Conservatives' attempts to gain control of the money supply, the foreign exchange rate for sterling became a variable that the Conservatives added as an explicit concern for the authorities. The 1982 Budget included this along with the PSBR and £M3 as the main instruments to be monitored for economic management. There may well be an explicit target for the exchange rate, though this has not been publicly announced and is denied by the authorities. Clearly there would be some difficulty with announcing an exchange rate target. Such an announcement would immediately create conditions in the market where pressures and speculations around the target would arise and serve to undermine it. It is also not clear that the authorities would be able to prevent this. But the addition of at least a monitoring of the exchange rate goes to confirm the continued commitment of the government to 'intervene' in a wide range of markets and circumstances, even if this is just to smooth out fluctuations.

However, the framework in which any such intervention might take place is now fundamentally different to that of the 1950s/60s and even up to the mid 1970s. The most important difference concerns the fact that currencies now float against each other. Fixed exchange rates were abandoned in 1972. In fact this is less important than is sometimes admitted because the currencies that really matter in the context of the world economy are restricted to a relatively few OECD countries. The central 'blocks' here are the US$, Sterling, the EMS currencies (which are largely linked to the German Deutsche Mark and the French Franc), the Swiss Franc and finally, to a lesser extent the Japanese Yen. It is the relationships between these five currency 'blocks' that really count so that the economically significant rates are relatively few.

However, this still puts the authorities very much on the defensive as there is little they can do against any sustained movement either in or out of their currencies. In the UK context all outstanding exchange controls were further abandoned by the Conservatives in 1979.

In addition to this fundamental change, an important adjunct concerns the growing inter-dependencies between the financial centres of the world that developed during the 1970s along with the development of 'offshore' financial centres and funds (like the 'Eurodollar' and 'Eurocurrency' markets). This has meant the successive integration of a widening range of financial, capital and money markets in different countries and the entry of a wider range of agents into external currency dealings. The whole of the financial community is now 'ultra-exchange rate sensitive', as well as a growing number of large and medium sized manufacturing and commercial companies.

A number of implications arise from these developments. In the first place this means that the management of a domestic economy 'behind' a relatively fixed exchange rate is now no longer possible. It also means that there is a limit, instance, on the PSBR/GNP ratio that can be tolerated in any one country. It would not be possible for this to get too far out of line with the ratio in other countries before speculation and other pressures arose against the currency of the particular country concerned. This is most acute with respect to the weaker economies like the UK. But it also means that it is now virtually impossible for any Left government to borrow its way out of a depression in isolation (as France has recently found). The large current deficit to GNP ratio of the US is only sustainable because of the still dominant position of the US economy, though even here there are clear signals that political pressures are building up against the US from European countries, because of the outdrain of capital to the US economy that this implies (and which was discussed in the previous chapter in respect to the UK).[1]

A second point to make here concerns the implied massive systematic increase in uncertainty in economic decision making that these and other changes have given rise to. This is one of the most significant developments during the 1970s. It has shifted the contours in which economic calculation

Figure 3.1: Economic Decision Making Cycle

Economic Conditions	Period of Decision Cycle						
	Less than annually	Annually	Quarterly	Monthly	Weekly	Daily	Several times a day
Low inflation and fast growth (1950s–1970)	exchange rates; investment	wages; product prices	stocks; labour force; interest rates	commodity prices			
high inflation and little growth (1970–1980)	investment	investment	product prices; labour force; stocks; wages		commodity prices; interest rates		exchange rates
decelerating inflation and low growth (1980– ?)		product prices; wages	investment		commodity prices; stocks; interest rates; labour force		exchange rates

Key:
- 'monetary' variables
- 'real' variables
- instability

Source: Adapted from The Economist September 24th 1983 'World Economic Survey' p.11.

must take place and a range of fundamental
practical and theoretical problems have been thrown
up in its wake. This in turn displays a number of
features, one set of which is illustrated in Figure
3.1. Here the periods between which typical
economic decisions have to be made are illustrated
under three sets of economic conditions. Both
'real' and 'monetary' elements are involved and
there is the added dimension of the 'instability'
in some of the variables to which businesses must
react.

With conditions of high inflation and little
growth the spectrum of economic activity about
which decisions have to be made shifts to a much
quicker and unstable regime, led by the exchange
rates. With decelerating inflationary conditions,
one or two of the decision variables have moved
back to a more settled state, though the 'real'
features of stock levels and labour force have
become relatively more unstable. Overall it is the
exchange rates which display the most dramatic
change and this itself has had feedback effects on
a number of the other features illustrated in the
figure. This figure is only meant to be illustrative
and no doubt there could be arguments about the
placing of particular features, though it does show
the rough character of the tendencies involved.
Perhaps the most striking general feature of the
period from the early 1970s has been the way
monetary variables have become more uncertain and
unstable. The US money supply figures are now
announced on a weekly basis (4.10 pm every Friday)
and interest and exchange rates react quickly to
these. (UK money supply figures are released on a
monthly basis with similar reactive consequences.)

One of the important effects of the growth in
volatility with respect to the foreign exchange and
domestic monetary markets has been the growth in
the phenomena of exchange rate overshooting. With
flexible exchange rates and rapidly altering
exchange rate expectations and perceptions a good
deal of 'noise' can be created in international
exchange markets which leads to the 'over-reaction'
of the market to any domestic disturbance (and
which may imply non-equilibrating financial markets
- see below p.70). As a result exchange rates can
fluctuate more violently than the underlying
position might warrent. Table 3.1 shows various
measures of the sterling exchange rate over the
period of the Conservatives' administration. The
first column shows the nominal exchange rate

48

against the US dollar. The second column shows the 'effective exchange rate' - this represents a single measure of the relative price of the pound against a large number of other currencies - weighted with respect to the significance of the UK trade with the countries concerned. Finally a measure of the 'real' exchange rate is given in the final column. The nominal and the effective rates measure the price of the pound relative to foreign currencies. The 'real' exchange rate measures the price of UK goods relative to the price of foreign goods - in this case adjusted for unit labour costs.

The main point to be drawn from Table 3.1 is the way the exchange rate appreciated between 1979 and 1980. This large and rapid appreciation propelled the economy into an even more alarmingly uncompetitive position internationally and as a result added significantly to the domestic recession. To a large extent this effect in the foreign exchange market was predicted by the Conservatives' announcement of the MTFS in 1979, and their relative tightening of domestic monetary policy. Expectations at least, were altered and re-formulated by this move, which had its implications in the foreign exchange markets. However, to be fair to the Conservatives, the extent of this appreciation was probably unforeseen. Thus a largely unforeseen 'overshooting' took place which added significantly to unemployment and a reduction in domestic output, but this was hardly an explicit policy objective of the government itself. It would be wrong, therefore, to attribute all of the rapid increase in unemployment that took place in the early 1980s simply to a deliberate policy on the part of the government, though there is little doubt that it used the resulting effects to its own ends.

In fact just this kind of 'overshooting' was happening to the US dollar during 1984 when it appreciated very rapidly, particularly against European currencies. This increased the uncertainty on the part of European governments as they feared the consequences of a rapid fall of the dollar when the extent of the 'overhang' became apparent in the markets. This illustrates the way that exchange rates have become particularly volatile under floating regimes, how there is little individual governments can do about this, and how increased uncertainty in terms of unforeseen developments and consequences are generated in this context.

Table 3.1: Sterling Exchange Rates (Annual averages)

		1975 = 100	
	Against US Dollar ($)	Index of Effective Exchange Rate Against Weighted Bundle of Currencies	Trade Weighted Index of Exchange Rate (Includes Unit Labour Cost Adjustment)
			(Approx)
1978	1.92	81.5	108
1979	2.12	87.3	139
1980	2.33	96.1	160
1981	2.03	95.3	143
1982	1.74	90.7	140
1983	1.52	83.3	133
1984	1.28	77.7	130

Sources: Compiled from the various editions of BEQB, NIER and The Economist.

As Table 3.1 shows sterling became much more competitive against the dollar during 1982 and 1983. Its trade weighted position also improved relative to 1980. But a slightly wider perspective needs to be brought to bear here if an important point is not to be missed.

In popular discussion it is the Dollar/Sterling exchange rate that is highlighted and stressed. But in fact this is much less important than the Sterling/European currency exchange rates. The reasons for this are illustrated in Table 3.2. This shows the relative disposition of UK exports to various country groups over the period 1973 to 1984. What should be highlighted from this table are the relative importance of North America (mainly the USA) and of Europe as the destination of UK exports. North America has been declining (or at best stable) in significance, while Europe has increased its share, particularly the EEC. Over half of total UK exports are now destined for European countries, so it is the exchange rates here that are crucial to price competitiveness.

Table 3.2:   UK Exports 1973-1984 - Distribution Between
Countries

	% Total	EEC	EFTA	Total Europe	North America	Developing Countries
		Developed Countries				
1973	74.6	32.5	12.7	45.2	16.0	21.6
74	74.1	33.5	12.8	46.3	14.0	22.3
75	69.5	32.6	12.1	44.7	12.1	26.7
76	70.8	36.0	11.5	47.5	12.3	25.9
77	70.2	37.0	11.6	48.6	11.9	26.6
78	69.8	38.6	10.2	48.8	12.0	27.0
79	74.6	43.0	11.3	53.3	11.8	22.2
1980	74.5	43.4	11.8	55.2	11.3	22.4
81	73.5	41.3	10.8	51.3	14.0	24.0
82	74.5	41.6	9.6	51.2	15.0	23.5
83	76.8	43.8	9.7	53.5	15.4	21.1
84	78.5	44.8	9.5	54.3	16.2	18.9

Source: NIER August 1985 Table 16

During the early 1984 period, while Sterling
depreciated significantly against the Dollar, it
held up firmly against most of the European
currencies (except the German Mark and Swiss Franc)
and even appreciated relatively against some of
these others for a time. Thus Sterling became
relatively less competitive against its European
partners, other than Germany and the small Swiss
economy. Of course to some extent this movement
should be reflected in the trade weighted indexes
of the exchange rates shown in Table 3.1 but here
there is a problem of updating the weights and
these measures not allowing for trends in the
direction of trade flows. As a result they
overestimate the improvement in the exchange rate
position in recent years. The 'improvement' in the
position of the US in 1983/4 is due to the
appreciation of the US dollar against Sterling

which has given an unexpected and probably temporary boost to UK exports to the USA. In late 1984 Sterling not only depreciated further against the dollar but did so also against the main European currencies.

A further important and interesting consequence of the quickening pace of economic decision making and the growth of uncertainty surrounding this have been attempts to deal with that uncertainty by developing and extending markets into new areas. All calculation relies upon some form of 'discounting' of the future by rendering it into a comparability of the present. Attempts are made to 'displace' the uncertainties arising with the future by developing means of forward contracting that might help to stablise the system. Example of such forward contracting are 'forward markets' and 'future markets' and these have been rapidly developing in the post 1970s era with respect to monetary and particularly exchange rate phenomena.

Forward markets (along with 'spot markets' - markets in which buying and selling is for immediate delivery) have long existed with respect to both commodities (mainly raw materials and agricultural products) and some financial instruments. Where there is uncertainty about prices in the future 'forward contracts' can be struck to 'hedge' against the risks involved. The trader who hedges deliberately eliminates the possibility of a gain in order to safeguard against a possible loss. In the foreign exchange area this allows companies to predict with certainty the domestic currency equivalents of future receipts or outgoings in foreign currency. For example, an exporter may approach a bank to sell forward dollars which he or she expects to receive in a month's time. Or those with investments or debts denominated in foreign currencies can use the forward markets to eliminate exchange rate risk by selling their prospective receipts in advance at a known exchange rate.

What has developed more recently, first in the US and now in the UK are 'financial futures' markets. In the wake of high inflation and exchange rate floating, businesses have been forced to treat as variable certain costs which previously had been regarded as relatively fixed in nominal terms (see Figure 3.1). In the US it is now possible to engage in futures trading with respect to stock indexes (portfolios of shares and stocks) as well as a wide variety of other financial instruments and currencies. In the UK a London International

Financial Futures Exchange (LIFFE) was set up in September 1982 offering contracts on interest rates (Sterling 3 month time deposit and long-dated gilt-edged security rates, and Eurodollar 3 month time deposit rates) and in Sterling, Swiss Franc, Deutsche Mark and Yen to US Dollar currency exchanges. A further development was the opening of a Stock Index Futures market in the UK in 1984. In the US these markets have flourished (Financial Times November, 1983 and March 5, 1984). These developments in the UK are closely tied up with attempts to re-confirm London as the centre for international financial dealing in the 1990s, which is taken up again in Chapter 5.

Financial futures differ from forward markets in that entering into a futures contract does not guarantee the buyer the <u>current</u> market price, rate or yield but rather will be denominated in terms of what the seller <u>expects</u> the price or yield to be when the contract matures. Both parties thus have to make some judgement about what the expected price or yield may be at the contract maturity date before they would wish to enter a contract. With future markets both partners are literally trading on the future in terms of their expectations. These contracts are not means of ensuring that prices or yields at a future date will be what they are now. They are only means of ensuring that they can be <u>known</u> now.

A question that these kinds of market raises is whether systemic uncertainty is genuinely reduced or whether it is simply redistributed around the 'players' according to their different <u>ex-ante</u> expectations, the action they take based upon these and the <u>ex-post</u> outcome. Is someone's gain simply offset by someone else's loss in a zero-sum form? Clearly if overall uncertainty <u>is</u> reduced there is some net gain in terms of output (or 'welfare') that would not otherwise be produced. That there are gainers and losers in speculative markets is beyond doubt though the conditions under which a net gain emerges (or where some party has to bear the cost) is something that cannot be developed in this book.[2] In the next section, however, we look at an area of current economic controversy where this general problem is acutely posed. This concerns the implications of the 'debt crisis' facing many less developed economies that has arisen in the late 1970s and early 1980s, in the wake of a range of international financial developments.

53

3. THE LDC DEBT PROBLEMS

One of the major problems to emerge in the context of the world economy during the recent recession has been the continual debt repayment difficulties that LDCs in particular have had to cope with. While this does not immediately affect the Thatcher Government's own internal economic strategy it does impinge upon it in as much as the UK economy is caught in the web of financial dealings that have accompanied these problems and in the various political 'initiatives' (or 'non-initiatives' according to many) that have surrounded the difficulties in re-scheduling the LDCs' debt. The spring 1984 leading nations economic summit held in London was only one of a number of such events which addressed this issue (or perhaps failed to address it).

This general issue becomes much more important for the UK in terms of policy initiatives when the question of the LDC debts are put into the context of moves towards an economic recovery (Roe et al 1984). The LDCs occupy a very important source of demand for UK exports, as Table 3.2 showed. The share of these going to the LDCs is greater than that going to the USA, so a recovery in this latter economy is perhaps less important on this score than avoidance of any further deflation of the economies of the LDCs. The LDCs as a group provide a massive trade surplus for the UK (for instance a positive balance of £2.1 billion - £0.277m excluding OPEC - over the twelve months ending in August 1982 - see Roe et al 1984 Table 1 p.102). What kind of a solution emerges for the LDCs' debt problems is thus of a very much greater overall significance for the prospects of the UK economy than is often recognized.

The debt problem needs to be put into context. In the first place while it is a widespread problem for the LDCs as a whole it is a critical problem for only a relatively few of these. The main actors in the drama are the three Latin American countries of Brazil, Mexico and Argentina. These, along with Colombia, Venezuela, Peru and Ecuador, had outstanding debts of over £350 billions at the end of 1983. The major creditor was the USA, or more accurately a number of large US banks. The growth in the exposure of US Banks to the LDCs' as a whole is shown in Table 3.3. In June 1983 this amounted to $207 billion and, perhaps more importantly this represented over 200% exposure on their capital base. The table also makes the point that these problems have not just appeared in the last year or so but have been building up throughout the 1970s, and even before. The loan exposure of particular US banks to Brazil, Mexico and Argentina are shown in Table 3.4. Again it is the extent of the loans to a very small group of countries compared to the banks capital base (stock equity) that has caused most concern amongst commentators. We return to this in a moment.

A second point to make about the context of this problem is that any economic agent is expected to borrow (become a debtor) during a period of development or capital formation. The LDCs have been no exception to this and have been net debtors on capital account during most of the post Second World War period. The issue became a 'problem' when, for various reasons, creditors became uncertain about the ability of debtors to repay their loans. One measure traditionally used to identify this possibility is 'export cover'. For Mexico and Brazil in 1983 for instance debt repayment obligations amounted to over 100% of their export earnings and for Argentina this ratio had reached 137%. This put the question of the necessity to re-schedule some of these debts firmly on the economic and political agenda. But what have been the underlying reasons for the emergence of this kind of repayment difficulty? There are a number of determinants here which it will be worth quickly detailing.

In the first place the oil-price escalation of the mid 1970s left a number of the non-oil producing LDCs with substantial balance of payments disequilibrium on their <u>current</u> accounts. These LDCs found it politically and economically very difficult, if not impossible, to adjust their internal demand and consumption pattern sufficiently quickly to accommodate the new situation. Secondly, the general recession itself had depressed the exporting ability of the LDCs to exploit markets in the MDCs as much as they might otherwise have done. In addition it had stimulated protectionist tendencies within the MDCs which had a dispro-portionate effect on LDCs' exports (eg the Multi Fibre Agreements with respect to textiles discussed in greater detail in Chapter 5). Thirdly the period witnessed a switch from official funding of LDCs' balance of payments disequilibrium to private funding of these. The large commercial banks, particularly American commercial banks, became

Table 3.3 Exposure of Nine US Banks to LDCs

		Total Foreign Claims ($bn)	Claims on Non-Opec LDCs ($bn)	As % of Assets	As % of Capital
1977	Dec	132.7	30.0	8.1	163
1978	June	135.9	31.0	8.0	164
	Dec	147.3	33.4	7.9	176
1979	June	151.8	35.0	7.8	166
	Dec	168.2	39.9	8.2	182
1980	June	176.7	41.9	8.2	182
	Dec	186.1	47.9	9.0	199
1981	June	196.0	51.6	9.3	206
	Dec	205.0	57.6	10.2	220
1982	June	209.5	60.3	10.6	222
	Dec	205.3	64.2	10.9	221
1983	June	207.4	64.4	11.1	213

Source: Country Exposure Report, Federal Financial
Institutions Examination Council.

Table 3.4: Loan Exposure of Top 5 US Banks to Main Latin
American Countries at end of 1983 ($m)

	Share-holders Equity	Loans to			Loans as a % of Stock Equity
		Brazil	Mexico	Argentina	
CitiCorp	5771	4600	3000	na	132
Bank America	5136	2484	2741	na	102
Chase Manhattan	3051	2560	1553	800	161
Manufacturers Han. Trust	2671	2130	1915	1321	201
J.P. Morgan	3069	1785	1174	741	121

Source: _Financial Times_ June 4 1984

heavily involved in financing Latin American and other countries' balance of payments deficits. The sheer weight of finance involved overwhelmed official institutions like the IMF and World Bank and made it impossible for these to provide sufficient funds. At the same time, in a period of rapid institutional change on the world financial markets in which credit creation escalated, backed by inflationary domestic monetary conditions and large deposits from oil-producing countries, the conditions were set for the commercial banks to increase their lending to willing, or in some cases 'desperate' customers. The final main point is one that emerged critically in the 1980s as the leading developed economic nations began their own adjustments to the inflationary conditions of the 1970s and 1980s. Interest rates began to rise in an attempt to prevent domestic monetary growth and, in the case of the US economy, to finance its budget deficit. The increase in 'real' interest rates, as inflation began to be checked, placed an added burden on debtor countries in their attempt to re-schedule their loans from commercial banks. It was during this period that the banks found themselves significantly 'over-exposed' with respect to some of the Latin American countries. Where their capital base was not sufficient to cover the outstanding loans, those banks involved became highly vulnerable to the threat of default. Banking works on confidence and is highly interdependent as between different institutions. Continental Illinois (America's eighth largest bank) got into acute confidence difficulties in May 1984 with between $2 billion and $3 billion outstanding loans to LDCs and had to be 'bailed out' by the US government. This speculation triggered a number of other large US banks included in Table 3.4 which were in an equally exposed position.[3]

To some extent the problem for a number of the large debtor countries is the sheer size of their debt, rather than their 'export cover' as mentioned above. Absolute amounts have become the issue rather than, say, debt to GDP ratios or debt to export earnings ratios, which have traditionally been used to assess the credit worthiness of countries (although these kinds of ratio are still important, particularly for the smaller debtor countries). In addition the problem of 'capital flight' has been significant. It is estimated, for instance, that as much private capital left

Argentina during the early 1980s as was needed to cover its 'official' balance of payment deficit.

Capital left this and other countries even in the face of real exchange rate <u>appreciation</u>. Despite very high levels of domestic inflation the exchange rates appreciated and private capital was invested abroad in the face of expected devaluations, domestic deflation and restrictions, and the general instability surrounding these likely policies.

One other important issue that has raised a good deal of comment concerns the reasons for continued high money interest rates in the US economy. Other than the existence of a large budget deficit mentioned in Chapter 2 perhaps the crucial point here is the fact that interest payments in the US can be deducted for tax purposes by both corporate and individual tax payers. Thus the net of tax interest rate is significantly lower than the gross money rates. However, what is the case in the US economy is not symmetrical with respect to other economies and this leads part way to an explanation for what is seen as an 'intolerable' interest rate burden on the LDCs compared to its relatively more mild effects within the US itself. This has also led to a discussion of the ways in which this problem might be dealt with on a world scale, notably some form of interest rate capping for the LDCs' debts.

Questions of reform of this major world problem fall into short-term measures and longer-term measures. Both involve or imply some structural re-adjustment on the part of the LDCs and the international financial system, though it is the exact combination of where the main 'burden' of the adjustment should lie that is the subject of intense political dispute. As far as the shorter-term adjustments are concerned rather familiar IMF backed policies are in predominance. These stress a return to monetary and fiscal orthodoxy on the part of recalcitrant governments to reduce internal budget deficits, cut backs on public expenditure and money supply in the anticipation that such 'deflationary' procedures will help right the balance of payments disequilibrium by depressing internal demand and imports and stimulating exports. These kinds of responses are linked with agreements that if such a policy is pursued the rescheduling of debts will be more favourably looked upon, easier terms and conditions applied, etc. Such an 'imposed' solution was essentially that concluded with Mexico in 1983/84. Exactly what form the re-scheduling actually takes and should take is the subject of widespread debate. The normal case is for a lengthening of the time period of repayment and/or the spreading of the risks between a wider group of private commercial banks with some explicit official institutional support; in effect to subsidise such re-scheduling. In addition various 'rate-capping' suggestions have been made such that that part of the commercial banks debt involved with financing only the LDCs' balance of payments deficit could be floated at a lower interest rate than current market rates via specially endorsed bonds. Again this suggestion implies a subsidy to the country in question, indirectly mediated through the private banks dealing with it. Clearly here lies the political problem since some country, someone or some institution must bear the cost of these schemes. Most of the suggestions that are front runners in international financial circles effectively socialize, in one way or another, these burdens and so far have, in effect, socialized them amongst the tax payers of the advanced industrialized economies, at least immediately.

Both the Right and the Left response to this has been to suggest it is far from satisfactory. On the one hand it is argued that the LCDs themselves should shoulder much more of the burden (in addition to taking their deflationary medicine). This has been the main argument emanating from the intellectual Right. It is associated with a commitment to greater 'liberalization' of international trading and investment arrangements with the countries in question, trying in particular to extract concessions associated with direct investment in some of the resource base of their economy. This would imply investors of the industrialized countries taking a more extensive equity base in the productive sector of the LDC economies, backed by guarantees against possible nationalization of these interests in the future. On the other hand the Left (and to some, though lesser extent the Right also) has argued that the commercial banks themselves should bear the burden of the adjustment. This would mean their profits taking the strain, or if more drastic measures were called for, that they should issue more shares or bonds to increase their capital cover and thereby shore up confidence. This would mean that it would be bank shareholders who would 'bear the cost' of their own organization's mismanagement of its financial affairs, in a normal commercial manner. In fact there is evidence that bank share prices in the US were being written down by the Stock Exchange over the period of the most acute banking crisis in 1983-84 and that the banks were expanding their capital base by liquidizing some assets, thus producing a financial 'loss' to existing share-holders.

What is interesting about these longer term suggestions for structural change is that the world leaders have been proceeding ultra-cautiously with respect to them - led by Margaret Thatcher and Ronald Reagan. In effect this amounts to support for the status quo of a combination of IMF deflationary initiatives for the LDCs plus modest official support for the commercial banks in the metropolitan countries. The hope is that the problem will rather simply wither away as the promised recovery gathers momentum.[4] A piecemeal, case by case approach is in order in the interim, with added 'scrutiny' by the IMF and possible greater World Bank involvement. This latter organisation is to be brought in to help with a longer-term investment strategy, to lessen dependence on private bank finance. But its commercial wing, or a newly established fund, is to take the brunt of this, confirming a basic market oriented desired solution. The two leaders mentioned above in particular have squashed calls for a significant increase in Special Drawing Rights to be made available to the IMF, to extend its emergency and medium term financial support for severe disequilibrium cases. Such a development would 'delay', it is argued, the necessary internal adjustment that the affected LDC economies need to make. The main cost, it would seem, is thus to be borne once again by the people of the LDCs, and to the lesser and uncertain extent by US taxpapers. This hardly amounts to a radical solution since it re-confirms the entire post 1945 trajectory in these matters.

It also leaves unsolved the major structural problems that gave rise to the problem in the first place. Given the way the commercial banks have burnt their fingers in a really massive way over their financing of the LDCs deficits, this source of finance is unlikely to re-emerge strongly in the future. Confidence at a world level has been severely shaken and is likely to take a very long time to become fully re-established. If this is the case, other sources of finance for the LDCs need to be found even if a 'recovery' of sorts does take place. Clearly one way of providing this alternative source of finance would be for non-bank direct investment to develop once again. But this is fraught with political difficulties. The selling of a large share of some LDC productive capacity to foreign investors is unlikely to be very appealing to the governments involved, or even to potential investors given present political instabilities in most of the countries concerned. Without some new official and probably multi-lateral initiative and involvement this would not seem a serious alternative, but such multi-lateral involvement is effectively what is being ruled out by the dominant voices in the leading industrialized countries (though it must be said that France and Canada have voiced different and more accommodating views).

Another way of 're-adjusting' the situation would be to 're-patriate' the capital spirited overseas by wealthy citizens and institutions during the run up to the 1983-84 re-scheduling crisis. Quite how this could be done is not at all clear but at a minimum measures might be implemented to restrict any further 'capital flights' of this kind. These would involve tight exchange controls within LDCs in general, though possibly also restrictions on the acceptance of deposits by the major commercial financial institutions as well. However desirable these kinds of measures might be in the abstract, they are both unlikely to work and unlikely to be implemented in the present climate of opinion. They are unlikely to work because such a mechanism could not be successfully introduced on an ad hoc, one to one country basis, but would have to involve a near universal coverage in terms of countries and authorities if it were not to be easily and continually circumvented. International financial markets are now so closely linked and interdependent that individual initiatives would simply not work. In addition, they are unlikely to be implemented since the dominant climate of opinion supports the increased 'liberalization' lobby even if this, in effect, means a protection of already entrenched and sectional interests.

One other direction for possible reform would involve a properly co-ordinated and directed attempt to both stablize exchange rates and reduce real-interest rates differentials, combined with a modest reflation at the world level. In effect this would mean a major and far reaching multi-lateral

61

accommodation between the highly industrialized economies themselves, and in turn between these and the LDCs. It would also have to involve something akin to the re-establishment of a post-war fixed exchange rate regime. Whilst there are plenty of suggestion and policy initiatives available in this context they are again unlikely to be acted upon, for much the same reasons as outlined above. In the absence of a really major and uncontrolled (or uncontrollable) collapse of the world financial system any accommodation along such lines are ruled out politically at present. Such a collapse remains only a very remote possibility and certainly not something to be welcomed. In the absence of this the course followed is likely to remain an ad hoc and partial one, involving variations on the mechanisms of possible reform outlined above. Instead of political decisions being made about which group or groups should or could bear the burden and cost of the necessary readjustments and then designing a scheme to meet this, essentially ad hoc and partial re-active mechanisms will be generated, the distributional consequences of which will only become apparent as things work themselves out.

One final point in this section concerns an issue already mentioned above in connection with the absolute amount of certain countries' debts. Because large countries tend to have large absolute debt levels they are likely to find themselves at a disadvantage compared to smaller countries. There is anyway a presumption (and in fact some evidence) that smaller more culturally homogeneous countries, can adjust more easily and quickly to external economic constraints than large diverse and heterogenous ones. Countries like Hong Kong, Singapore, the Phillipines, Taiwan, South Korea etc. (other things remaining equal of course) are those going to find themselves more favourably placed than India, Brazil, Argentina, Nigeria, etc. This may have profound consequences for where further economic development can take place in the last two decades of this century, and also on the status and stability of those large countries themselves.

4.   THE ROLE OF RATIONAL EXPECTATIONS AND MARKETS

It is in the context of both the increase in uncertainty and the formation of new markets to respond to it that a number of crucial theoretical developments have taken place in economics. One of the more formidable of these is the rational expectation's 'revolution' of the 'new-classical economics' (NCE) which emerged in the mid 1970s. This lays great stress on the way expectations are generated within market structures. Such rational expectations go to re-confirm the basic price adjustment mechanism of the Walrasian framework in situations of increased uncertainty. In formal terms the rational expectations hypothesis, as it is called, is discussed in the appendix to this chapter.

This theory assumes economic agents are rational utility maximizers (or profit maximizers) and will not make systematic errors in their judgements about future prices or other variables. On average, barring unforeseen random events, any expectations formed about prices will be correct so that economic agents will have no reason to revise the process by which expectations are formed. This is rather convenient for economic model builders since it implies that agents will form their expectations about the future 'as if' they were in command of the appropriate (rationally constructed and specified) model of the economy and its trajectory.

Turning to the policy implications of rational expectations in the context of the Conservative MTFS, the idea here would be to announce a firm money supply target and to stick to it. This money supply target would translate itself into a definite expectation of the general rate of inflation or price formation (given the assumption of a known and definite link between the money supply and price formation in a monetarist manner). All agents' expectations of prices would then be fixed in terms of a definite outcome. The 'problem' of inflation would thereby be solved.

In effect what this theory of rational expectations suggests is that government fiscal policy aimed at increasing the level of employment would not work. It would only result in added inflation. Supposing the government embarked upon an expansionary fiscal policy. At first the money wage rate is unchanged but prices begin to rise as a result of the increased economic activity, so that real wages fall. Consequent upon this firms demand more labour and output expands. But if workers expect their real wages to fall as aggregate demand increases they will immediately 'discount' the government action and demand higher money wages. Such higher money wages will in effect maintain their real wages constant but result in an increase in the price level. In addition if real wages are held constant in this manner firms will not demand more labour or produce an increase in output so real output will remain the same and not be increased by the fiscal policy. Thus demand management under those assumptions defeats itself and results in added inflation only.

In the UK this kind of position has been taken up most strongly by a team of economic modellers based at Liverpool University under the direction of Patrick Minford, (though it is also strongly represented amongst econometric model bulders at the London Business School). The former have consistently produced assessments and forecasts of the economy which have shown highly optimistic results and predictions, (e.g. Minford, 1980). Minford has also more recently defended the deployment of this form of analysis in the area of modelling the labour market (Minford, 1983). Here it is assumed that agents generate their expectations about wage formation along the lines following rational expectation assumptions (which assumes flexible prices and wages). Thus given an announcement of the money supply growth, workers would 'know' as well as anybody else what the subsequent rate of inflation would be and would adjust their bargaining position appropriately. All this is something that many other economists have found difficult to accept - particularly those who support the idea of a 'non-flexible' price regime in the labour market. Wages are not as flexible downwards as the rational expectation theorists might think, it is argued, and nor is their upward flexible primarily dependent upon expectation formation in the manner outline above.

The New Classical Economics presents itself as a universal theory of price formation in an economy in general. Its strong presumption is that all economic agents form their expectations 'rationally' in essentially the same way in all markets. Given that NCE is a 'dynamic' variant of Walrasianism it is tempting to repeat the criticisms levelled at its counterpart in the micro-sphere, i.e. neo-classical economics, concerning its individual-istic, essentialist and subjective basis. But this is to miss the point of a more differentiated response which is sensitive to the particular conditions prevailing in individual markets. To condemn it out of hand in a general manner is to fall into a similar trap that the theory lays for itself.[5] Each 'market' or 'area' of the economy should be scrutinized in terms of whether a 'rational expectations' approach represents a credible and feasible method of modelling its particular activity. It is in the light of this approach that the idea of rational expectations modelling can be evaluated more adequately.

Accepting this approach, it would seem unlikely that the mechanisms of the labour market and wage bargaining in the UK are amenable to serious assessment in the context of rational expectations suppositions. Whether one likes it or not the rigidities built into the system via an extensive unionized labour force and through developed 'internal labour markets' (where the redeployment of labour and promotions are not subject to market assessment and criteria) would work to undermine its applicability. Even if agents did form their expectations 'rationally' there is no clear way in which they could make these felt, given collective bargaining and the hiring practices of firms. Workers already within firms have no mechanism by which they could 'offer themselves' at different prices, even if they wanted to.

Wage bargaining in the UK displays a highly complex structure. As a result a very fragmented pattern of pay settlements emerges. The main determinant of pay deals still seems to be some combination of the actual rate of inflation and the ability of firms to pay in terms of their profit levels. This differentiated response has itself been encouraged by the growing decentralization of wage bargaining mechanisms. Firm and plant level bargaining has been displacing national or industry wide bargaining procedures. But even so there are still some large areas, particularly in the public sector, where national bargains continue to be struck and in the private sector the momentum for decentralization seems to have slowed down considerably. In fact any further 'decentralization' could turn out to be a recipe for major problems in the longer term as it could encourage familiar 'leap frogging' and 'wage drift' with the emergence of economic recovery. As it stands however public sector bargaining is itself characterized by a range of 'comparability' procedures and assessments which are not strictly market orientated. Here, in addition, long-term pay deals are on the increase

(these are also to be found in the private sector).
In addition minimum wage legislation still covers
some 10% of all employees (2.7 million low paid
workers) in both the private and public sectors.

All this complexity in what is still a
basically collective bargaining structure mitigates
against any easy way in which a general expectations
procedure can be seen to apply. In addition there
is a massive lack of any agreement amongst
economists over the way money supply levels affect
prices, let alone a widespread appreciation of this
amongst the working population at large. Under such
conditions if expectation formation and bargaining
is based upon a desired _real_ wage on the part of
workers - as seems likely to be the case under UK
conditions - then 'rationally expectant' workers
would be involved in generating expectations about
the spectrum of relative prices for _all_ other goods
and services in the economy, as well as of their
own 'price' for wage labour. The information
requirement here would be quite formidable and
beyond most agents' capacity.

The argument is then to be sceptical about the
appropriateness of 'rational expectation' assumptions
for most of the labour market. There may be pockets
of a differentiated and non-aggregative labour
market in which conditions for the formation of
expectations approach 'rationality', so that its
assumptions could form the basis for a working
calculation. This could be the case in certain
sections of the construction industry where casual
practices such as the '_lump_' are still strongly
represented. But overall actual conditions mitigate
against its widespread deployment.

However, this does not mean that the approach
need be rejected _in toto_. There are markets in
which rational expectation assumptions could form a
much more credible working hypothesis. The money
and foreign exchange markets are cases in point.
Here information is widely and quickly disseminated.
It is more or less available in the same form to
all agents in the market at the same cost. Under
these conditions both spot and forward/future
markets would seem to work reasonably 'efficiently'
given the limits of their applicability. Here
expectations about future price movements, whilst
complicated in their formation, might not be
seriously at odds with something approaching
'rational expectation' conditions. (Though see the
next section where a different approach is outlined
in the context of disequilibrium conditions). What

is being suggested is thus a much more differentiated approach to the framework for modelling the economy overall, in which more attention is paid to the particular (institutionalised) conditions, mechanisms and practices typifying different 'markets' or aspects of economic activity.

In this respect it should not be forgotten that the case Muth (1961) had in mind when developing the first set of arguments about rational expectations was that associated with agricultural output. The argument was pitched in the context of two theoretical precursors. One of these was 'inventory speculation' models and the other a long debate in the literature about the status and effectiveness of 'cobweb' theories. Ezekiel (1938) developed the first 'cobweb' model with an expectation therorem, basing prices in the current period on simple extrapolation of prices in the previous period. Muth credits Nerlove and Arrow with first developing the adaptive expectations procedure around agricultural price formation (Nerlove 1958; Arrow and Nerlove 1958). In contrast to the classic cobweb model, where farmers expectations differ from the model predictions such that farmers' do not learn from experience - i.e. disequilibrium persists - with the adaptive schema (as discussed in the Appendix), forecasts of prices change by an amount proportional to the most recent observed forecast error. In these models instability can still exist, which requires a price support programme for agricultural produce, and it is this kind of a result that rational expectation theorists chide and want to avoid. Cagan (1956) was the first to deploy adaptive expectations to purely monetary phenomena in the context of general price setting.

Against these models Muth develops an approach based on what one can only surmise were ideas about how something like the Chicago Wheat Market works.[6] But the Chicago Wheat Market deals with a product with a one year production cycle. Thus the effects of price formation in this kind of a market are likely to be different to an activity which demonstrates perhaps a three to four year production cycle, as do many other agricultural products. But a more decisive point is to recognize that the moment of price formation in wheat and frozen orange juice futures, or in 'pork belly' futures is a peculiarly restrictive kind of market. It is highly institutionalized, dealing in a relatively homogenenous product, having a limited

number of more or less equally well informed
traders, etc. It is not even like a localized,
information deficient and highly differentiated
small scale market for pigs in some mid-Western
market town.

The trap Muth fell into here was to
'generalize' his analysis too far, substituting the
conditions pertaining in something akin to an
auction market for a relatively undifferentiated
product, for the conditions of the economy as a
whole. This is a trap that many subsquent theorists
seem to have fallen into including those at
Liverpool and the LBS. The wheat or 'pork belly'
futures markets might display a reasonable
approximation to rational expectation conditions as
might some financial futures markets; the labour
market does not nor does the market in real capital
goods, and nor does the economy as a whole.

5.   LEAVE IT TO THE MARKET?

Markets have always been celebrated for the
efficient way in which they make use of information
and in times of uncertainty such presumed
characteristics are at a premium. But there is an
even more general problem that needs to be
confronted here. This can perhaps be best
illustrated by reference to the way the market
mechanism as a whole tends to be treated within
orthodox economics, and particularly by certain
American economists. These themes have been
strongly taken up by the Conservative Government -
at least rhetorically - in the early 1980s. What is
invoked here is the 'market' as the prime virtuous
mechanism which is to be stimulated at the expense
of the 'public' or 'political' provision of goods
and services. Some have seen this as the main issue
being faced in the current situation. A strong
proponent of this position is Milton Friedman:

> In the economic market - the market in which
> individuals buy and sell from one another -
> each person gets what he pays for. There is a
> dollar for dollar relationship. Therefore you
> have an incentive proportionate to cost to
> examine what you are getting. If you are
> paying out of your own pocket for something
> and not out of somebody else's pocket, then
> you have a very strong incentive to see
> whether you are getting your money's worth.

The Exchange Rate, Markets and Uncertainty

The 'political' mechanism, on the other hand, displays a 'fundamental defect' in that:

> ...it is a system of highly weighted voting under which the special interests have great incentive to promote their own interests at the expense of the general public. The benefits are concentrated; the costs are diffused; and you have therefore a bias in the political market place which leads to ever greater expansion in the scope of government and ultimately to control over the individual. (Friedman 1976 p.10)

Here are a familiar set of themes in which the market dispenses benign <u>discipline</u> whereas the state or political allocation dispenses ultimate <u>oppression</u>. But the interest of these remarks from the point of view of the argument here is the presumed symmetry between the 'market mechanism' and the 'political mechanism' that they embody. These are simply different means to accomplish a well defined and homogeneous end. They are judged in respect to a common rationality of individual calculation - compared and contrasted in terms of this meta-discourse. But in fact the two mechanisms are quite distinct, both in terms of their purview and their mode of operation, which undermines a simple juxapositioning of their respective legitimacies in terms of a presumed singularly dimensioned rationality. They need to be judged, as a result, on separate criteria, specifying the appropriateness and limits of each. Each general mechanism brings into play quite a different set of social forces and calculations and it is only in terms of these that objectives can be properly considered and assessed.[7]
Similar considerations pervade the analyse of the market system itself. Here, there is a danger with the abstract idea of 'a market' as such. The invocation of a general 'market mechanism' always avoids the actual detail of how specific markets work and the constraints and limits that operate on them and through them. Some of these highly institutionalized mechanisms may work roughly according to the principles of 'rational expectations', others will not. As a result any analysis of the 'price mechanism' is only 'rational' in a limited sense - with respect to a definite pertinence and set of material conditions of existence. Thus while markets are conventionally looked at as displaying

69

a general and universal character, it is perhaps more fruitful to conceive of these as always particular in character and institutionally set. As this chapter has already demonstrated - and which we shall further discuss below - a number of new markets have been developed over recent years in the context of financial and monetary relationships and these go to demonstrate that markets are always created. They are not a 'natural' feature of economic life but are always actively promoted and planned for. The institutional mechanisms through which such markets work then provide the context in which expectations and uncertainties are generated and exist and can be calculated.

Clearly 'rational expectations' theorists are committed to the idea of market clearing. When pushed such a position denies that there can be any involuntary unemployment in the labour market. Any unemployment of labour is largely the result of a choice on its part between work and leisure. This combines with the idea that what unemployment there is is determined 'naturally' (the 'Natural Rate' hypothesis) by the underlying capacity, competitiveness, growth and technological condition of the economy. In the face of this there is little if anything governments can do in terms of fiscal policy to try to stimulate economic activity beyond its natural level. Such activity on the part of government only results in inflation rather than any real growth in output. Such positions are clearly overtly reactionary. With some 35 million people currently unemployed in OECD countries it seems unlikely that these are all in this position by choice.

There has however been quite a different and probably more fruitful theoretical reaction to the emergence of increased uncertainty and new market structures in the monetary field. This builds on a concept already well developed with respect to stablization policies and forward markets. In these areas various 'buffer stock' mechanisms have been developed in an attempt to iron out fluctuations in what is recognised to be non-clearing market systems. What this position has done is to take up the idea that money or financial markets - including the foreign exchange markets - might not clear and be in an instantaneous equilibrium. This has led to a growing literature on what is termed 'buffer stock money' or 'disequilibrium money'. (See Laidler 1984, Goodhart 1984 Chapter X, and Bain and McGregor 1983 for recent summaries and discussion). With this approach money holdings, and even a wider range of financial instruments, are held in part as constituting a buffer stock to be deployed in dealing with emergencies, unforeseen changes in economic conditions and shocks, etc. Economic agents are not, then, thought to re-adjust continuously their full economic dispositions but allow any shocks to impinge, at least initially, upon certain liabilities or assets which act as buffers.

Whilst this might seem a fairly obvious idea it has important implications for the specification of demand for money functions and for the control of money supply via interest rate manipulation. Perhaps the most important effect, however, is to give an added theoretical space within orthodox economics to the idea that markets do not clear and to generate a new concept of money to specify this. It can also help give some more theoretical precision to the phenomena of exchange rate overshooting discussed in Section 3. This is probably more fruitfully looked at in terms of a disequilibrium form of analysis than in terms of a 'rational expectations' equilibrium approach.

6. DEVELOPMENTS IN THE CAPITAL MARKETS

It now remains to say something briefly about the capital market developments in the UK. The chief point to make here concerns the relative demise of the Stock Exchange as an important source of new investment funds for industry. This was particularly depressed over the period of the late 1970s and early 1980s largely because of domestic depression and low profitability levels. In 1983, however, there was a resurgence of activity mainly asociated with rights issues. These expanded in the context of established firms re-organising their capital structure and gearing ratios. These had become skewed during the period of rapid inflation in the late 1970s. By making a rights issue the firms involved substituted share capital for loan capital.

By and large the Stock Exchange is now a market for government debt and a secondary market for the re-arrangement of portfolios amongst the financial institutions. As can be seen from Table 3.5 - which shows Stock Exchange turnover for representative months in 1983/84 - some 80% of its business is involved with financing government and

71

other public bodies, debt. While Stock Exchange indicators like the Financial Times Share Index appear to be a pre-eminent measure of the strength and state of the economy, their real significance is minimal in this respect. They operate rather as a 'sign' only of the state of the economy. Even the new issue business of the Stock Exchange is dominated by the public sector. Between January and June 1983 the nominal value of new public sector business was £10,815 millions, while the UK companies accounted for only £1,890 millions, much less incidentally than the figure for foreign companies at £6,872 millions. These tendencies may be upset in the near future as large floatations of equity develop, associated with the present Government's de-nationalization programme. This programme is discussed in detail in Chapter 7.

Table 3.5: Turnover of UK Stock Exchange: (Percentage of total by value)

	Dec 1983	April 1984	July 1984
British Funds:			
Short dated (under 5 years)	42.4	45.5	39.1
Others (over 5 years)	33.5	22.3	41.2
Irish Funds	3.1	5.6	3.3
UK Local Authorities	1.5	1.7	0.8
Overseas Government	0.5	0.6	0.5
Other Fixed Interest	0.8	1.3	0.8
Total Official Funds	81.8	77.0	85.7
Ordinary Shares	18.2	23.0	14.3

Source: Stock Exchange Monthly Business Release (various months)

Attached to the Stock Exchange is the new Unlisted Securities Market (USM), which was opened in November 1980. This is essentially a market for venture capital - 226 small companies having been floated on it at the end of 1983 with a capitalized valued of some £2 billion (compared to fully listed companies, value of some £150 billions). The setting up of the USM was a response to the demise of the Stock Exchange new issue business. It allows small and growing firms to come to the market without having to meet the stringent and expensive requirements applied to a full listing. Turnover on the USM was nearly twice as rapid as on the listed market in 1983 confirming the greater speculative character of this market.

In fact more external investment capital was raised through leasing agreements by companies between 1980 and 1982 than was raised by the issue of new securities on the Stock Exchange. Leasing has grown from the mid 1970s into a major form of investment finance for companies. The reasons for this are mainly associated with the tax advantages associated with this form of finance in periods of low profitability. (The 1984 Budget has now eliminated many of these tax advantages, see Chapter 7). It also reflects a response on the part of companies to the increased uncertainty typifying commercial life. It has given them flexibility akin to 'buffer stocks' in the face of shocks and unforeseen emergencies. Lessees pay the equivalent to a rental for their equipment or plant and credit risk is shifted to the lessor (mainly commercial banks). Rentals are paid out of current income and this avoids the necessity and expense of raising large amounts of capital for investment outlays.

During 1984 the Stock Exchange was going through a major re-organisation as far as its practices of operation are concerned and this is looked at in more detail in Chapter 5 where the Conservative 'liberalization' initiatives in this area are discussed.

7.   CONCLUSIONS

To sum up on this chapter we can say that it has shown how new markets have been set up and developed during this period of the late 1970s early 1980s. But these have been largely outside of the purview of Government policy and would have developed even if Mrs Thatcher's government had not been elected. (Except, perhaps, for the current transformation of the Stock Exchange). The period has been one in which uncertainty about economic activity increased significantly. These developments, along with a re-emphasis on the 'market mechanism' in general and on particular markets, is a response to this. They open up a wider range of <u>options</u> for economic agents. It is also in this context that theoretical developments need to be set. We have seen how rational expectations arose as a response to the increased uncertainties generated largely by changes in the international and national financial parameters with respect to which economic agents make their calculations about the future. Thus we should view both the growth and celebration of the 'market mechanism', and certain of the more important theoretical developments associated with it as grounded in these material conditions. These provide the framework in which the policy initiatives discussed in the following chapters need to be understood and assessed.

Appendix : Rational Expectations : A More Formal Exposition

Rational expectations can best be illustrated in the context of trying to model the inflationary process. Inflation can be specified simply as follows:

$$P_t - P_{t-1}$$

This simply states that inflation is the difference between the general price level, P, in period t as opposed to the previous period t - 1.

Expectations about the rate of inflation can then be written as:

$$_{t+1}P^*_{t-1} - {_t}P^*_{t-1}$$

This expresses the character of the rate of inflation between periods t and t+1, expected at the end of the previous period, t-1. (P^* now specifying expected price levels).

The question is posed as to how these expectations are formed. There are two general responses - 'rational' expectations and 'adaptive' expectations. These provide the means for representing the problem of the public's ('psychological') expectations of the price level that is thought to be going to prevail in the next time period, this expectation being held at the end of the previous time period, i.e. $_{t+1}P^*_{t-1}$ With 'rational' expectations this can be specified as:

$$_{t+1}P^*_{t-1} = \left({_{t-1}}P_t + 1 \right. \quad ------------(1)$$

In (1), the term $_{t-1}P_{t+1}$ provides a mathematical expression for all the probability distributions and information about prices in the next period, held at the end of period t-1 (Muth 1961). Thus with rational expectations there is a kind of 'instantaneous' adaptation of expectations to all the information about actual prices as inferred from the previous period. They are inputed from the formal structure of the model. All the information available is shared equally by all economic agents to construct their own expectations (or probability distributions associated with these). If they then act 'rationally' and consistently on this information and expectations they cannot be 'wrong' about them. The expectations will not be 'unrealized' and in the aggregate the expected price level is an unbiased predictor of the actual price level. In this case then the 'future' can be inferred as a known probability distribution from the immediate past. It is only when 'exogeneous' shocks or 'irrational' behaviour intervene that this smooth progress and process is interrupted. Such 'irrational' behaviour is usually associated with governments and trade unions - both in effect issue 'false' information. The policy burden of 'rational expectations' is thus to eliminate these irrational-ities as far as possible. This is discussed in the main text.

The other expectations procedure is one governed by a distributive lag or adaptive scheme:

$$_{t+1}P^*_{t-1} = \sum_{i=0}^{q} V_1 \, P_{t-1} \quad \text{------------(2)}$$

In (2) the parameter V_1 is a fixed number varying between 0 and 1. The equation says that the expectations about prices in the next period held at the end of the previous period are equal to a summation over all the commodities in the market of the prices prevailing of those commodities at the end of the previous period, subject to the factor of adaption V_1. In this case then 'actual' future prices will lag behind expectations by a factor dependent upon the value of V_1 which is a weighted average of past prices. Since in the following periods this adaptive scheme may change, actual prices need never meet expected prices. There is only a tendency towards actual prices meeting expected prices, which is continually being re-cast in terms of the lagged actual prices becoming the basis for new expectations of prices - it is a geometrically weighted <u>moving</u> average. If the lagged structure were to remain of the same form i.e. V_1 in this instance taking the same value as V_2, V_3....V_n, then actual prices and expected prices would asymptotically approach one another. The values of the Vs thus settle the rate of adaptation of expectations about prices. The value of the Vs would have to be established empirically.

Clearly the rational expectations procedure involves a basic demand and supply model supplemented by an 'intergenerational' expectations formulation, where what is crucial is the informational content of prices, which is correlated as between periods. Only prices enter into the information on which firms and other agents adjust both 'over' the period and 'between' periods. In fact the period is defined as that over which prices are in equilibrium and they rationally adjust <u>between</u> periods. This effectively renders any actual 'period' into an instant with no duration. Strictly speaking it is not a period, say, over which investment adjusts to an equilibrium. This and any other information available to agents only affect their expectations about what will happen in the future. In effect this collapses Marshall's 'long run' into the 'short run' by imposing a fully specified theory on any data set. This eliminates questions of genuine 'uncertainty' and collapses these into questions of 'risk' (in Knight's sense - see Hoover 1984).

Notes

1. Mrs Thatcher has herself led these complaints (Financial Times December 9 1983)

2. For some interesting and accessible analysis of this if in a slightly different context see Casson (1982) Chapters 5 and 12.

3. While the UK banks are not as heavily involved as US ones substantial sums have also been lent. Their loans to Latin America stood at $23 bn in 1983 with the UK heavily committed to Argentina ($4 bn outstanding loans). Export cover was also thin, with Midland and Lloyds debt to equity ratios running at 189% and 195% respectively in 1983.

4. Confidence in this approach has been drawn from the likely emergence of a trade surplus of some $20 bn for Mexico and one of $6 bn for Brazil in 1984.

5. Such is the case with Helm's (1983) recent and otherwise interesting critique. There is by now a formidable literature both _pro_ and _con_ with respect to 'rational expectations'. For sympathetic surveys see Kantor (1979) and Berg (1982). The critical camp has been on the defensive but Tobin (1983) probably offers the most influential and consistent opposition from a neo-Keynesian position - see also Mayes (1981). Post-Keynesian writers have been consistently critical of NCE but they have tended to conduct an out of hand form of critique and rejection which mirrors the New-classical positive case in its generality. The latter provides an argument _for_ a method of modelling the economy overall whereas the former reject this claim on logical or epistemological grounds, but also on an all or nothing basis. See Davidson (1982) and Gomes (1982). The most accessible recent survey along the 'pragmatic' lines developed here can be found in Shaw (1984)

6. This is partly confirmed by a look at the references cited in Muth (1961).

7. Chalmers Johnson (1982) shows clearly how 'plan-rationality' and 'market-rationality' differ in the context of Japanese industrial policy.

References

Arrow, K.J. and Nerlone M., (1958) 'A Note of Expectations and Stability' Econometrics, Vol XXVI p.297-305.
Bain, A.D., and McGregor, P.G., (1983) 'Buffer

Stock Monetarism and the Theory of Financial Buffers', University of Strathclyde Mimo.

Berg, D.K.H., (1982) The Rational Expectations Revolution in Macro-Economics: Theory and Evidence, Philip Allen, Oxford.

Cagan, P. (1956) 'The Monetary Dynamics of Hyperflation' in M. Freidman (ed) Studies in the Quantity of Theory of Money, University of Chicago Press, London.

Casson, M. (1982) The Entrepreneur: A Economic Theory, Martin Robertson, Oxford.

Davidson, P. (1982) 'Rational Expectations: a Fallacious Foundation for Studying Crucial Decision-making Processes' Journal of Post-- Keynesian Economics Vol V No.3 pp.182-198.

Ezekiel, M. (1938) 'The Cobweb Theorem' QJE Feb, Vol.11 pp.255-280.

Freidman, M. (1976) 'The Fragility of Freedom', Encounter, November pp.8-14.

Gomes, G.M. (1982) 'Irrationality of Rational Expectations', Journal of Post-Keynesian Economics, Vol V No. 1 pp.51-65.

Goodhant, C.A.E. (1984) Monetary Theory and Practice: The UK Experience MacMillan, Basingstoke.

Helm, D. (1983) 'Informational Assumptions and Rational Expectations: A Critique'. Money Study Group Conference, Oxford, September 1983.

Hoover, K.D. (1984) 'Two Types of Monetarism' Journal of Economic Literature March Vol XXII pp.55-76

Johnson, C. (1982) MITI and the Japanese Miracle, Stanford University Press, California.

Kantor, B (1979), 'Rational Expectations and Economic Thought', Journal of Economic Literature, Vol 7 pp.1422-41.

Laidler, D (1984) 'The "Buffer Stock" Notion in Monetary Economics', Supplement to the Economic Journal, Vol 94 p.17-34.

Mayes (1981) 'The Controversey over Rational Expectations' NIER No 96 May pp.52-61.

Minford, A.P.L. (1980) Memorandum to Treasury and Civil Service Committee, Monetary Policy Vol II, Minutes and Evidence, HCP 163 II Session 1980-81, London, HMSO.

Minford, A.P.L. (1983) Unemployment: Causes and Cure, Martin Robertson, Oxford.

Muth, J.F. (1961) 'Rational Expectations and the Theory of Price Movements' Ecomometrics Vol 29

No 3 pp.315-35.
Nerlore, M. (1958) 'Adaptive Expectations and Cobweb Phenomena' Quarterly Journal of Economics, Vol 72 pp.227-240.
Roe, A., Renshaw, G., and Ahmad, E. (1984) 'The International Aspect to Britain's Economic Recovery' in Warwick University Department of Economics, Out of Work: Perspectives of Mass Unemployment.
Shaw, G.K. (1984) Rational Expectations, Harvester Press, Brighton.
Smith, K. (1984) The British Economic Crisis, Penguin Books, Harmondsworth.
Tobin, J. (1983) Neo-Keynesian Monetary Theory, Basil Blackwell, Oxford.
Williams, K., et al (1983) Why Are The British Bad at Manufacturing? Routledge, London.

Chapter 4

THE SUPPLY-SIDE WITHIN A MACRO-FRAMEWORK

1.   INTRODUCTION

The previous chapters have concentrated upon the
more macro, monetary and financial aspects of the
Conservative Government's economic policy. In this
and the following chapters the focus is upon the
micro aspects and upon the 'real' sectors of the
economy. This will involve a closer look at the
issue of personal incentives, at 'privatization',
de-nationalization and 'liberalization', at
industrial policy and at conditions in the labour
market and such like.
      The Conservatives' overall strategy is seen to
have two dimensions. The first involves 'monetarist
macro-economics' broadly speaking where the
emphasis has been on controlling inflation via
controlling (or trying to control) the money
supply. The second aspect involves an attempt to
re-kindle the output growth and the working of the
industrial structure via a set of policies designed
to increase competition and personal incentives and
initiatives - the withdrawal of government
intervention and regulation of detailed sectors of
the economy, the reduction of taxation, de-nationalization, etc. This latter aspect is sometimes
referred to as the 'supply-side' of the economy.
Indeed there is a whole new school of predominantly
American economists who have developed a distinct
theoretical position around some of these issues.
This is known as 'Supply-Side Economics' (SSE).[1]
This position gained a great deal of credence
because of its early influence on President
Reagan's economic policy making. (David Stockman,
former Director of the Office of Management and
Budget, and a close adviser of President Reagan, is
credited as being heavily influenced by SSE.)

Reagan's first budget was seen as being in many
ways a classic supply-side document - emphasising
tax cuts and the withdrawal of government
interference in the market economy. This was to
herald a 'dash for growth' in which the resulting
significant increase in output would enable the US
economy to shake off any inflationary and
unemployment problems. While such a 'dash for
growth' on the basis of a supply-side prognosis has
not been fully attempted by Mrs Thatcher's
Governments, the general position has been strongly
endorsed by a number of its advisors and has
appeared regularly in ministerial pronouncements.
At the level of rhetoric, it is a strong element in
the government's thinking.

   As we shall see below in this chapter, such a
supply-side position cannot simply be treated at
the micro-level. It involves a number of
macro-features as well. Indeed the framework for
discussing this general position, developed in
Section 4, is explicitly macro in character. Whilst
the emphasis taken from this framework is a micro
one the analysis itself involves a combination of
macro and micro features.

2.   THE SUPPLY-SIDE POSITION - AN INITIAL
     SPECIFICATION

The background to SSE stems from a reaction against
Keynesianism with its emphasis on 'demand
management'. Keynesianism is demand sided, it is
argued, and neglects or ignores the supply side of
the economy. It stresses the manipulation of the
components of aggregate demand to regulate the
economy and assumes that whatever the level of such
government stimulated demand, the supply to meet
this will be forthcoming without producing serious
economic problems. Supply-siders, however, challenge
these assumptions. They argue that subsequent
growth in the size of the government budget and
extent of government intervention in the economy
will produce inflationary pressure, but also a
moribund and inflexible supply position. They are
particularly concerned with the conditions of
labour supply in this context, to which we return
below. In general terms however the idea is to put
strong downward pressure on the input costs of
production, i.e. to increase the cost competitiveness
of the economy.

   The struggle between these positions involves

a number of doctrinal disputes which are not without their importance, and these are further discussed in the next section. But it is also important to recognise that this dissatisfaction with the emphasis on a Keynesian demand management macro-economic framework stems just as much, if not more, from the way it has 'performed' in the context of trying to manage the UK economy since 1945. One of the continually re-occurring problems has been that when demand was stimulated the expansion of the economy soon came up against supply-side bottlenecks and constraints. The failure of domestic supply to adapt quickly enough usually resulted in a sudden upsurge in imports to fill the supply gaps so created, and this engendered a subsequent balance of payments disequilibrium. The expansion then had to be halted to right the balance of payments position. This sluggishness of supply adjustment is a further reason for concern with it in a policy context.

An interesting feature of SSE particularly in the American context is the way it has become predominantly associated with conditions in the labour market and with taxation and welfare benefits. Clearly a renewed focus on the supply-side of the economy could extend to a number of structural features involving the character and composition of the capital stock, its vintage and sectoral composition, the general state of technology, the organization of production, and on managerial and financial conditions etc., i.e. with the industrial structure overall and with the finance of investment, broadly conceived. By and large these areas have not formed a focus for SSE in the USA though they have been much more important in the UK. In Chapter 7 we shall discuss this in terms of the Conservative Government's industrial policy in the early 1980s.

By and large though the emphasis from SSE has been on the supply of labour involving the supposed disincentive to work effects of taxation levels and of income maintenance and support measures, and with the effects of a heavily 'monopolized' trade union organizations. These features will have the effect of forcing the general price level up as output expands, it is argued, largely because higher wages will be demanded to compensate for higher taxation and a monopolized labour force will be able to extract such a price from employers. In addition these features will distort the tendency for price flexibility downwards in the labour market during periods of recession and unemployment. Indeed, in the absence of such 'price' flexibility in the labour market, unemployment will be higher than it need be in times of recession. In that case the conditions which underlie such 'inflexibility' are the causes of unemployment and should form the objects of government policy in this field. It is clearly only a short step from this to the idea of reducing taxation and welfare benefits to stimulate individual initiatives and to the reform of trade union practices to reduce their 'monopoly power'. (The Conservatives' initiatives with regard to the trade unions are discussed in the next chapter.) In addition more widespread de-regulation of the economy and even its 'de-nationalization' can conveniently be associated with these arguments, in the name of increased private incentives more generally. Such at least in outline is the theory.

3. THEORETICAL ARGUMENTS AROUND THE SUPPLY-SIDE POSITION

One of the main theoretical planks that underlies the resurgence of supply-side economic arguments is Say's Law. J.B. Say (1767-1832) was a French economist working in the nineteenth century and a popularizer of Adam Smith's economic doctrine of the 'invisible hand' in his native France and on the Continent more generally. While there is some dispute as to whether Say actually fully formulated his 'Law' (some would suggest that James Mill was its real originator e.g. Spengler 1945) it is generally agreed that he had formulated most of its central components by the time the 1819 edition of his book '_Traite d'economie politique_' was published (Say 1834). The classical economists in England popularised Say's Law and developed it (Ricardo, McCullock and Mill, in the main).
What, then, is Say's Law? Put rather starkly it states that 'Supply creates its own Demand'. Here we can see its immediate interest for 'supply-side' economists. If we concentrate upon the supply-side, demand will take care of itself. This seems immediately to undercut Keynes' emphasis on effective demand as the real problem for the aggregate economy.
The logic of the Say's Law argument is that the level of production determines the level of demand in an economy. In one sense this is a rather trivial statement because it is clear that at the

aggregate level the value of all the income payments made to people as 'producers' (i.e. rents, wages and profits) is equal to the value of all the output so produced by them for sale. Thus these 'producers' would have enough income to purchase, as 'consumers', all the goods offered for sale over any time period, and _ipso facto_ the value of products equals the value of incomes - production or supply creates, or brings to the market, its own demand. In fact this particular formulation of what Say and the other Classical economists were saying is probably best expressed as Say's Identity and it is argued this is sometimes confused with what Say actually said and meant (Harris 1981 Chapter 6).

Say's _identity_, then, can be used to argue that under all economic circumstances aggregate supply will equal aggregate demand. Thus there can never be an overproduction of commodities nor an under consumption of them. That is, there can never be a general glut nor a general demand deficiency in the economy. If planned demand for goods equals planned supply in this way there seems no reason why national production and the national income derived from it should diverge from the full employment level. Thus real national income will always be at this full employment level. There can be no involuntary employment of resources under these circumstances.

Whether this was actually Say's (or the Classical economists') general position and therefore his Law is open to dispute. To a large extent it seems that the Law has been retrospectively attributed to Say - attributed to him in the form of an identity, thus 'reading' his position to generally support what is sketched above. In fact it seems that Say did acknowledge the existence of general gluts in the short-run and it was only over the long-run that he thought some 'automatic' adjustment mechanism would bring supply and demand back into equality. And this is the crucial point since it is _flexibility_ of prices that offers the mechanism by which this longer-run adjustment can take place.

Later economists of the neoclassical school in the main seized upon these arguments to make three main points in connection to it:

(a) Say's identity/law generally holds in the economy, so the main emphasis must be on attending to the conditions of aggregate production and supply.

(b) There can be no general and sustained involuntary under or unemployment of resources in a 'naturally' functioning economy.

(c) Prices must be flexible, and if necessary <u>made to be flexible</u>, so that short-run maladjustments to the equality of supply and demand can be quickly (and some would say 'instantaneously' e.g. those supporting the rational expectations approach discussed in the previous chapter) adjusted to equality.

Whilst Say's Law as formulated in this fashion, provides a general Classical and pre-Keynesian re-statement of the basic features thought to typify a capitalist economy, it is important to recognise that it does not of itself provide any particular policy suggestions for how to manage such economies. It simply invokes a rather general justification for 'price flexibility'. But it is with respect to this aspect that a number of more specific theoretical positions have been generated to support detailed policy arguments. There is a danger, then, of forcing all of the economic theory and policy of what is termed the 'New Right' into one homogeneous unity. In fact it is far from this. There are significant differences between monetarists and supply-side economists for instance over exactly how the price level is formed, even though both would pay lip service to the need for price flexibility.

Given the broad outline of SSE sketched above, the crucial element for this position in economic decision making is represented by the government's stance towards the taxation and income maintenance side of budgetary policy. Monetary policy and particularly 'monetarism' is less important from this point of view. Inflation, it is argued, is fundamentally caused by taxes, not increases in the money supply. Milton Friedman, for instance, is still a demand-sider - stressing the <u>active</u> role of money and supporting the 'quantity theory of money' (i.e. that it is the quantity of money in the system that largely determines aggregate 'demand' and the health of the economy in terms of production brought forward, and the level of inflation). For supply-siders money is <u>passive</u>. For them money automatically adjusts to the needs of trade; to restrict its growth will only dampen private sector initiatives and growth and ultimately contribute unnecessarily to _increasing_ inflation. Supply-siders, even though they may accept that the money supply can initially stimulate inflation, stress that it is tax increases which fuel it. It is the unremitting and relentless cultivation of the private supply of goods and services which provides the driving force to the economy and which can offset tendencies towards their public provision. Full play must be given to private sector inputs and creativity.[2] _Incentives_ are the major problem and it is tax reductions (along with welfare benefit reductions) which will provide these necessary incentives. Such reductions should not be confined to personal incomes however, but should also be extended to corporate taxation as well. Under these circumstances, the argument goes, firms will be willing to increase the amount of factor inputs they wish to employ and those factors will be more willing to become employed. The subsequent transfer of activity out of the 'hidden' or 'black' economy could even increase government tax revenue - despite the tax _rate_ being reduced. In fact it is _precisely because_ of this reduction in tax rates that government revenues will be increased. The approach stresses the role of high tax rates as generators of the 'black-economy'. Lower tax rates will re-stimulate legitimate economic activity, which then becomes subject to taxation. A benign multiplier effect on output growth could, then imply an increase in tax revenues for the government.[3]

This difference between the approach of SSE and 'monetarism' proper was seen by many commentators as being the major problem with President Reagan's 1981 budget. It posed the question of whether the tax reductions designed to stimulate economic activity would dominate over the 'Friedmanite' rule of a progressive reduction in the money supply which would act to deflate the economy and _reduce_ economic activity (Rousseas 1981-2, Fink 1982, Chapter 7). All this got quite complicated in subsequent years when a large budget deficit emerged. This was largely the result of the failure of the administration to control federal expenditures, particularly on the defence budget. What this goes to demonstrate, however, is the difficulty of attributing any actual economic policy simply to the dictates of a particular economic theory.

Nor is this distinction between 'monetarism' and SSE the only pertinent one in the policy context of the 'New-Right'. There exists an

'Austrian' critique of both of these. Monetarism for instance places its main emphasis on the <u>ability</u> of governments to control inflation and the economy more generally through controlling the money supply. In addition extreme monetarists argue that it is not the trade unions who create inflation but the growth of the money supply. Trade unions are powerless in the face of the 'natural rate' of employment. 'Austrians' like Karl Menger and Frederick Hayek would be highly suspicious of this. Government action of anything but a limited kind is not thought by them as desirable let alone effective. This is least of all with respect to economic regulation of an economy overall and at an aggregative level. For Hayek the main cause of inflation under contemporary conditions is precisely the trade unions and the monopoly power they exercise over the setting of wages. This position has argued for a 'short-sharp shock' of severe deflation to rid the economy once and for all of inflationary expectations, along with a legislative programme to dismantle the Trade Unions' privileges (Hayek 1978a). Hayek would like to 'de-nationalize' money altogether by allowing any agent to issue money. Money would then be constituted by any liability that the public expressed its confidence in by showing a willingness to hold (Hayek 1978b).[4] Under these circumstances the government would have no role to play in trying to control the money supply.

As far as the Austrian critique of SSE is concerned it focuses upon what it characterizes as the latter's pre-marginalist 'cost-sets-price' theory. SSE emphasized the incentives of 'producers' - it is production orientated. Supply creates its own demand almost in a classic Say's Law fashion. But this relentless cultivation of supply and the incentives associated with it rather ignores the consumer aspect of things, it is argued. Its (implicit) theory of value is 'cost-plus' related rather than being determined by consumer demand putting a value on output via the utility expected to be gained from its use. In distinction to the supply-side programme of an almost 're-industriali-zation at any price', the Austrian recommendation would be a programme of economic re-habilitation via the full elimination of the impediments to consumer choice which have largely been constructed by government legislation (Hazlett 1982). Supply-side type arguments can be easily employed to justify the use of government funds to rationalize the

productive structure for some 'presumed' longer
term benefit (like an 'industrial policy'), when
this should be left to the dictates of a
revitalized market mechanism with full consumer
sovereignty. It is but a short step from this to
the celebration of central planning, it is
suggested' (The Soviet Union is the quintessential
supply-side economy. Hazlett 1982, p.112.)

Whilst many of these arguments are not that
interesting or useful they go to demonstrate the
variety of positions being promoted. Nor do they
exhaust all of the possible variations - the
'economics of politics' approach could also be
elaborated in this context as a distinct position
itself (Tomlinson 1981, Thompson 1984). Clearly
these approaches share a great deal in common and
they overlap a good deal, but they all emphasize
something different as the main direction for
policy. They also generate conflicting policy
advice at times.

One obvious point they do share in common is a
basic celebration of the 'market-mechanism' -
something raised and discussed earlier in Chapter
3. However what exactly this 'market-mechanism'
means is now additionally differentiated along
quite distinct and theoretically complex lines. For
instance there is no clear agreement on this
between orthodox neo-classical economics and
Austrian economics. The former conceives of the
market in terms of a rather static equilibrating
mechanism - involving the general interaction of
suitably specified demand and supply schedules. The
latter on the other hand has a much more dynamic
and basically disequilibrium conception of the
market as a process. This is a process which is
forward looking, anticipatory and innovative (Dolan
1976; Kirtzner 1982). Thus it would be dangerous to
collapse all these approaches together around the
'market mechanism' unless account is taken of these
differences and their consequences.

4. A MACRO-ECONOMIC FRAMEWORK FOR SUPPLY-SIDE
    ADJUSTMENTS

In this section we develop a simple analytical
framework around which the discussion of supply-side
adjustments in subsequent chapters can be developed.
In this case the framework is explicitly macro and
aggregative in character, whilst the arguments
developed from

it have a more micro provenance. In particular the
focus will be upon the aggregate supply function.
It is policies directed to changing this that are
stressed by Conservative economic advice - rather
to the exclusion of possible changes in aggregate
demand, as mentioned earlier in this chapter.

The analysis takes the form of adjustments in
an aggregate supply/aggregate demand space, based
upon changes in the determinants of these
schedules. For those unfamiliar with the generation
of such schedules Appendix 3 at the end of this
chapter develops the argument in simple terms
around a usual textbook exposition. In the main
text below we look more at the policy context and
at the rationales offered for various desirable
adjustments to take place.

Before moving onto this, however, a word of
warning about the context of this kind of analysis
is worth making. The diagrams developed here rely
upon a good deal of economic theory which cannot be
properly developed in this chapter let alone this
book. In particular it assumes a working of the
economy which in many ways is quite out of step
with both how actual economics are known to perform
in general terms and with the type of conditions to
which the analysis is explicitly directed below.
Whilst the background conditions are assumed to be
equilibrating ones, in which markets are perfectly
adjusting, and so on, the conditions we are
actually dealing with are probably not adequately
expressed in these terms. The framework here is
also a 'Keynesian' one, in terms of how these
issues are discussed in orthodox accounts. However
the diagrams do offer a useful way of organising a
discussion and are meant only to be illustrative of
the kinds of issues at stake. The actual manner in
which the implied adjustments have worked out in
practice forms the subject matter of subsequent
chapters.

Let us now begin by exploring the consequences
of changes in the conditions of supply in context
of the diagrammatic framework developed in the
Appendix. As has already been mentioned, one of the
issues associated with supply-side economics
involves attempts to change the conditions of
production - to make production more efficient by
modernizing the capital stock, weeding out the
producers or upgrading the use of technology for
instance. All these issues are pursued in Chapter 7
which looks at the Conservatives' industrial policy
broadly conceived. Both of these adjustments can

be sketched in terms of parts (C) and (D) of Figure 4.4 in the Appendix. The aggregate supply function is generated from the interaction of the supply and demand for labour in the labour market and from the short-run production function. For the purpose of the analysis here we are only interested in the relationship between the aggregate production function and supply curve as depicted in Figure 4.1. We assume that conditions in the labour market are held constant and that the wage rate and price level are given.[5] To provide some purchase on the analysis two levels of labour use and price are sketched in Figure 4.1 as L_e, L_1 and P_e, P_1. These correspond to the same levels as shown in Figure 4.4 of the Appendix.

Changing the character of the capital stock or upgrading the state of technology is designed to have the effect of increasing labour productivity. In terms of the production function shown in Figure 4.1(C), this will push it out to the right. With the same level of employment as before a greater output can be achieved. We could either vary the capital stock or the state of technology independently or together. In either case the production function will shift to the right. In fact, in Figure 4.1(C) both K and T are assumed to have changed. The new production function is given as $Y = h_2 (L, \overline{K}^*, \overline{T}^*)$ where the * indicates the changed variable. It is clear that these changes have the effect of pushing national income Y_1 to Y^*_1 and Y_{fe} to Y^*_{fe}. The consequences this has for the supply function are shown in part (D) of the figure. In effect a new aggregate supply function is generated, AS_2. This involves a new full employment level of output at Y^*_{fe}.

Given this situation, whatever the position of the assumed stable aggregate demand function a higher output level for the economy would be generated with a lower general price level. This is a position that 'supply-siders' would clearly like to achieve.

We now come to a slightly more contentious part of the analysis. Here we look at the consequences of changing some crucial conditions in the labour market. In the first place we shall look at a rather artificial change - the effects of a reduction in the money wage rate schedule. Later we can combine this with a change in the supply of labour schedule itself. Both of these are quite crucial to certain strategies of supply-side adjustment which stress the labour market as

The Supply-Side Within a Macro-Framework

Figure 4.1: Changes in the Production Function

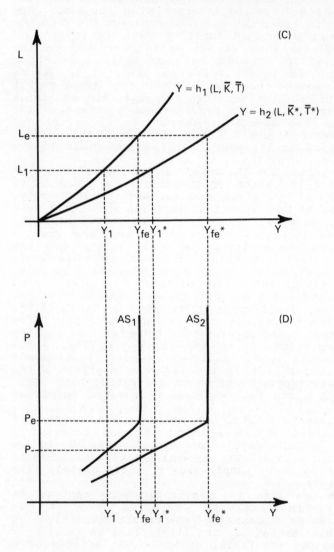

the central 'problem' of the economy.

In Figure 4.2, again drawn from the figure developed fully in the Appendix, we concentrate upon parts (B) and (D) of the diagram. The supply and demand schedule for labour are assumed constant, as is the production function. Supposing some change in the economy occurred or a policy was introduced that had the effect of reducing the money wage rate schedule from W_0W_0 to W_1W_1. This is shown in part (B). This is equivalent to a reduction in the general price level in that the same equilibrium in the labour market can now be maintained at a lower price level P^*_e. The equilibrium real wage rate does not change, $(\frac{w}{p})_e$, but it can now be sustained at a lower money wage rate since prices have fallen. The effects of this can be seen on the aggregate supply schedule drawn in part (D) of Figure 4.2. Prior to the change ASW_0 was the operative aggregate supply schedule. After the change ASW_1 is the appropriate schedule and this lies below the first schedule up to the full employment level. These changes do not then alter the full employment level of output, they only make the intra-full employment output less costly to produce. It is clear, however, that if the aggregate demand curve cuts the supply curve in this less than full employment area an increase in national income would ensue.

The final case to integrate into this analysis concerns direct changes in the labour market itself and their effects. In this case we maintain the assumptions embodied in Figure 4.2 about the autonomous reduction in the overall money wage rate but add to this an increase in the conditions of labour supply. In particular reducing the level of welfare benefits such that the ratio of income out of work to income in employment is decreased is supposed to stimulate the supply of labour. This ratio is termed the replacement ratio and the contentious arguments about its level and effects in the labour market are fully discussed in Chapter 6. However accepting the supply-side argument that reducing it stimulates the supply of labour, this would shift the supply curve from position S_0S_0 to S_1S_1 in part (A) of Figure 4.3. Other things remaining equal, this means that more labour will be supplied at any given real wage rate. Given the demand for labour characteristics specified by D_1D_1, this implies that a new real wage and employment level equilibrium is established at $(\frac{w}{p})_e^*$ and L^*_e respectively. Tracing these

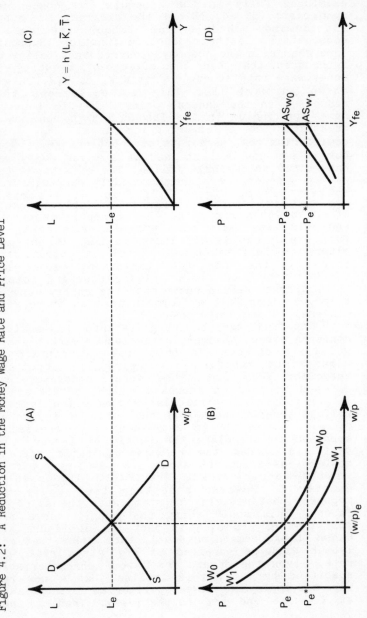

Figure 4.2: A Reduction in the Money Wage Rate and Price Level

Figure 4.3: A Full Labour Market Adjustment

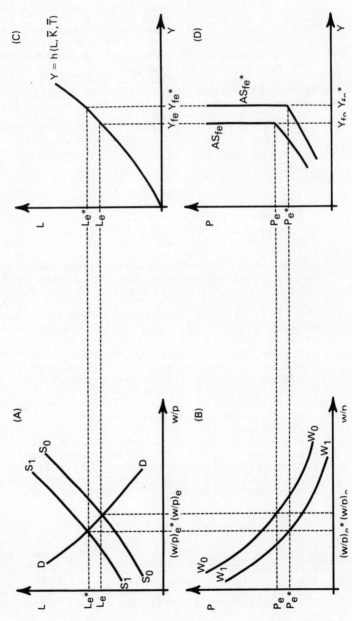

effects around the diagram produces a new full employment aggregate supply curve at AS_{fe}* which now lies wholly to the right of the previous supply schedule AS_{fe}. With <u>any</u> position for the aggregate demand schedule an increase in output and income is generated. It is these labour market adjustments that are discussed in a policy context later in Chapters 5 and particularly 6.

The main point about developing this analysis, then, has been to show how changes in the conditions of the labour market (pressures to reduce the money wage rate, increase in labour supply) and increasing the capital stock or upgrading technology can effect the position of the aggregate supply function. In particular we have shown how this can be pushed out to the right in the price-output space of part (D) of the diagrams. Given a stable demand function, a combination of increases in output and income and reductions in price level can be generated. Thus those who want to argue against 'demand management' can find in this kind of analysis a way of increasing income and output in the economy and of making it more 'competitive' by affecting the price level, without having to worry about adjusting demand conditions. Clearly this is its attractiion for market supply-siders.

The crucial issue this raises however is exactly <u>how</u> to engender these 'desirable' supply effects and what the wider consequences of them might be. It is in respect of this issue that quite different emphases and analyses emerge and quite different policy options are promoted. There is no general agreement on how best to engender a better supply condition for the economy but the dominant set of arguments representing the Conservatives' position concern the virtues of greater competition and market organised incentives. The specific forms that these have taken since the Conservatives gained office are discussed in later chapters. First it will be useful to develop the arguments at a more general level.

5.   A PROBLEM OF INCENTIVES

With respect to the question of competition and economic incentives, the argument goes that the economic decline of Britain is a result of the undermining and erosion of the elementary principles of free market capitalism through the growth of the welfare state, egalitarianism and a militant trade union movement. These are the end products of decades of domination by social-democratic ideology over all the mainstream political and economic tendencies during the Post-War period. The problem is to displace a paternalistic, bureaucratic state apparatus that has grown up around these tendencies and replace it with the renewed vigour of individual initiatives. This requires a withdrawal of state involvement from much of economic activity regulation and management, in the wake of which private economic initiative can grow and thrive. The re-defined role of the government is to provide the conditions in which individualized incentives of both workers and employers or entrepreneurs can flourish. To do this requires a two pronged attack - aimed at the two main areas of economic activity outlined above in the previous section which go to make up the conditions of supply in the economy i.e. the labour market and the structure of production, broadly speaking.

As far as the labour market is concerned a range of issues are involved here. As mentioned in Section 3, whilst some economists who argue along these lines recognise that wage demands by trade unions do not of themselves raise or lower the rate of inflation there must still be a strong resistence to excessive wage demands that outstrip productivity growth. Trade unions are directly responsible for the level of unemployment if they insist on a level of real wages which firms cannot pay. Trade unions are also responsible for stagnation and a slow rate of growth to the extent that they are capable of resisting rationalization, the introduction of new machinery, and the re-organisation of production and the labour process aimed at raising productivity. Thus these kinds of arguments are used to justify both a reduction in the 'monopoly power' of trade unions in the context of labour market adjustments and a resistance to higher money and real wages in the economy. Restraint on both of these fronts, it is argued, is vital to improve the supply condition in the economy and put downward pressure (at least) on many wages.

Of course the effects of high unemployment and stagnant or falling living standards might create pressures for an expansion of government expenditure and hence, it is argued, of the money supply. If government gives way to these pressures, higher rates of inflation will result. This is then another indirect result of trade union activity. The use of 'demand management' in this way is however doomed to failure from the point of view of this perspective because government efforts to realize a higher level of employment or a faster rate of growth by expanding demand falter in the face of a 'natural' rate of growth and a 'natural' rate of unemployment. These are themselves determined by the institutional organization of markets and other underlying conditions of the economy which manifest themselves in Say's identity working itself out in the long-run. Expanding demand can only raise the rate of inflation.

An additional element in this matrix of arguments against 'demand management' and for improving labour market supply incentives revolves around taxation. Pressures for demand managed re-flation under conditions of monetary stringency can lead to taxation increases to raise the necessary finance. This is to be avoided at all costs. Indeed the idea here is quite the reverse. Part of the pulling back of state involvement is to pull back on the taxation front as well. This is one of the main planks on which 'Supply-Side Economics' has been built as mentioned earlier and we shall be looking at this in closer detail in Chapter 6. Here it is sufficient to point out that reductions in the levels of taxation - whether corporate or individual - is again seen in the context of incentives to demand labour and to supply labour respectively. Put simply a reduction in taxation rate gives an incentive to employ more labour and for that labour to work harder, encouraging gains in real output, it is argued.

So much for the labour market arguments. What about the area of supply involving production characteristics and conditions more directly? Here there are also a number of issues that arise. One of the most important and controversial of these concerns attempts in the U.K. context to 'privatize' a number of the nationalized industries and other publicly owned corporate entities like parts of British Leyland and British Petroleum. This is explained in detail in Chapter 7. The argument here is that these organizations are basically inefficient in terms of their cost and productivity records compared to private industry equivalents (Pryke 1982, Beesley and Littlechild 1983). The conversion of these activities to private businesses will provide the necessary incentives for costs to be kept down and profitable operations to ensue. No longer will government subsidies be available. In the case of organizations like British Telecom and British Airways the aim is both to convert them to privately owned commercial operations as well as to open up a more competitive environment in which they would work by stimulating competitors (Mercury in the case of British Telecom) and de-regulating markets in others (allowing British Midland Airways or British Caledonian to compete with B.A. on a range of domestic and international routes for instance). In these cases the objective is to put downward pressures on costs by re-organizing the capital stock in the first instance rather than by increasing that stock overall. However it is confidently expected that this in itself will stimulate new investment in new technological fields, thus increasing the capital stock overall.

Added to these kinds of proposed measures can be a range of fiscal incentives. For instance special depreciation allowances and subsidies have been granted to firms who want to invest in new technological equipment of the 'robotic' and information technology type and even in other less glamorous investment areas (discussed further in Chapter 7). Also in the British context a range of fiscal and other incentives have been granted to firms who are prepared to set up in designated 'enterprise zones' mainly in rundown industrial and urban areas. Again the idea here is that if normal constraints and regulations can be lifted on private firms, they will seize the opportunity and stimulate real output.

In fact a whole ethic has developed about the 'small busiiness' in the UK and its supposed central role in economic recovery. Here the idea is that 'new technology' type investment and developments will better get started in the context of small businesses (such as Sinclair the electronics firm amongst others). What is invoked in this respect are the 'virtues of the entrepreneur'. A crucial role is allocated to the entrepreneur and to entrepreneurial spirit. What is needed is the 'vision' associated with such entrepreneurs who are prepared to take the 'risks' that larger and more comfortably placed corporate organizations shy away from. These are 'risk averse' - relying on their established business and market to maintain their relatively secured position. But in an uncertain world this will not do. Such a complacent attitude needs the stimulation and incentive of competition from the small dynamic

business sector which <u>creates</u> the opportunities
through its own natural (almost instinctual)
curiosity and imaginative quest for a profitable
combination of productive activities.[6]
Another of the important parts to be played in
this supply-side incentive approach is allocated to
the role of 'new technology': robotics, telematics,
information technology, bio-technology etc. The
rejuvenation and the renewal of the capital stock
and its more efficient cost effective organization
will require a replacement of the old inefficient
and rundown stock. As a prelude to this there is a
'shake out' of the existing productive capacity.
The idea here is that a leaner, thinner and fitter
economy is something of a pre-condition for the new
technology to take hold. This aspect of the
strategy is further explored in Chapter 7.

6.   CONCLUSIONS

In this chapter we have seen that there are a
number of elements involved in the economic policy
advice offered to the Conservatives, and indeed to
which they have chosen to listen. One result of
this is that often conflicting suggestions emerge
which are not always compatible. However, this does
amount to a strategy at least at a rather general
and suggestive level, involving more 'competition',
more 'de-regulation', greater personal incentives
etc. These elements comprise the 'policy promotion'
level and they are backed up by some often
conflicting theoretical advice. With respect to the
'policy implementation' level, however, we have yet
to see whether such policy promotion has been
effectively put into practice or indeed whether it
can be so deployed. While the main framework for
the analysis developed in this chapter has been a
rather standard macro-economic one, to pursue the
policy implementation consequences of this is to
move into a more disaggregated micro level. The
particular policy initiatives pursued in connection
with the stimulation of the 'supply-side' are
discussed in detail in the following three chapters
of the book. There we shall concentrate upon what
has actually transpired since the Conservatives
took office and look at some of the constraints
they have had to face and continue to face in their
efforts to promote their own particular approach to
economic intervention.
One final word is in order before we move on

into this analysis, which concerns the references made to the US in the above discussion. There are some fundamental differences in the way the 'New Right' has developed in the US and the UK despite obvious similarities between these. In particular one important and perhaps overriding difference is the relative absence of a concern with the connection between the PSBR or Federal Deficit in the US, and the growth of the money supply. In Chapter 2 this connection was discussed at length in the UK context, but by and large a similar concern has not been current within US economic policy debates. The Federal Deficit has been quite effectively 'de-monetarized'. More emphasis in the US has been placed upon the 'supply-side' programme and particularly the de-regulatory aspects of this. It has been such de-regulation along with the growth of the budget deficit and the stimulation of aggregate demand thathatit has implied was largely responsible for the significant recovery experienced in the US economy over the early 1980s. Whether this will soon come to an end when difficulties eventually emerge with inflation, as many commentators predict, remains to be seen.

The Supply-Side Within a Macro-Framework

Appendix: Constructing the Aggregate Supply Function

Generating the standard textbook aggregate supply and demand functions proceeds in the following manner. We can write an aggregate demand curve as:

$$p = f(Y, \overline{G}, \overline{M}) \quad (f_1 < 0, f_2 > 0, f_3 > 0) \quad (1)$$

where p = the aggregate price level
       Y = GNP
       $\overline{G}$ = Government expenditure (fixed exogenously)
       $\overline{M}$ = The nominal money supply (fixed exogenously)

$\overline{M}$ is in turn derived from the demand and supply of money functions:

$$M_d = M_d(p, Y, r)$$
$$M_s = \overline{M} \quad (2)$$
$$M_s = M_d$$

so that the money market is assumed to clear.

The product market is also assumed to be in equilibrium such that:

$$Y = C + I + G$$
$$G = \overline{G} \quad (3)$$
$$I = i(r, Y)$$
$$C = c(Y, r)$$

where r = the interest rate
       C = aggregate consumption expenditure
       I = aggregate investment

The aggregate supply curve can be written as:

$$p = j(Y, w) \quad (j_1 > 0, j_2 > 0) \quad (4)$$

where w = the money wage (which is derived as the inverse of the notional demand of labour).

The production function is:

$$Y = h(L, \overline{K}, \overline{T}) \quad (h_1 < 0, h_2 > 0, h_3 > 0) \quad (5)$$

where L = the labour force
       $\overline{K}$ = the given capital stock
       $\overline{T}$ = the given 'state of technology'

The profit maximizing firm employs labour up to the point

where $\dfrac{1Y}{1L} = \dfrac{w}{p}$ ----------------------- (6)

Thus from equation (5) and (6) we can write the aggregate supply curve. It is derived from the demand and supply of labour functions, together with the short-run aggregate production function. This can be represented diagramatically as in Figure 4.4 (Levačič and Rebmann 1982 Chapter 6). Supposing we have a demand for labour function of the form $L_d = a\left(\frac{w}{p}\right)$ and supply of labour of the form $L_s = b\left(\frac{w}{p}\right)$, i.e. that both the demand and the supply of labour are functions of the real wage rate $\left(\frac{w}{p}\right)$. These functions are shown in part (A) of Figure 4.4. Setting labour supply equal to labour demand to find the labour market equilibrium gives a labour employment of L_e and an equilibrium wage rate of $\left(\frac{w}{p}\right)_e$ shown in part (A).

In part (C) the short-run production function is depicted of the form $Y = h(L, \bar{K}, \bar{T})$ where $\bar{K}$ and $\bar{T}$ are the fixed short-run levels of the capital stock and 'state of technology' respectively. Thus here output is a function of labour input, (fixed) capital input and the (given) state of technology. With labour employment L_e, Y_{fe} results. This level of real output is consistent with full employment and equilibrium in the labour market.

Part (B) of the diagram shows what the real wage rate is for various price levels, given that the money wage rate is fixed at W_o. Under this assumption of a fixed money wage rate any level of employment below the equilibrium level L_e in (A) indicates a state of 'involuntary unemployment' for labour (an excess supply of labour). The real wage rate will be higher than the equilibrium rate and more labour would be prepared to supply itself under these conditions than would be demanded. Given a price level P_1 for example and money wage rate of W_o, $\left(\frac{w}{p}\right)$ is higher than the equilibrium rate and employment is lower at L_1. Tracing these conditions via the production function diagram shows that output and income would be at Y_1, somewhat less than the full employment level. The co-ordinates P_1, Y_1 give us a point of the aggregate supply function depicted in part (D) of the diagram. Other points on this function can be generated by varying the price level assumed. The aggregate supply function slopes upwards because as the price level rises with the money wage rate

Figure 4.4: Constructing Aggregate Supply

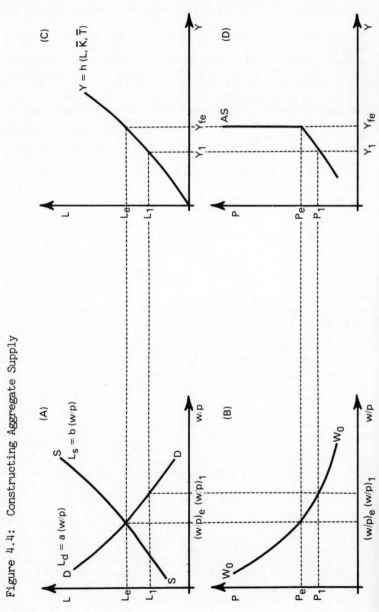

fixed the real wage rate falls. This stimulates employment and increases the supply of output at least up until the point where the excess supply of labour persists.

Once we over reach the position where the market clearing real wage rate is established at ($\frac{w}{p}$)$_e$ however, a situation of <u>excess demand</u> for labour would hold. Under these circumstances the real wage rate would fall <u>below</u> the market clearing rate. This would result in a decline in the amount of labour supplied and a subsequent decline in the level of output below Y_{fe} once again. In other words the aggregate supply function would bend backwards on itself at price levels greater than P_e. To prevent this happening it is usually assumed that the money wage rate becomes flexible <u>upwards</u> once the full employment equilibrium level of output is reached. In this case the aggregate supply function becomes invariant with respect to the price level and it becomes a vertical line as shown in part (D) of the diagram.

This analysis provides a basic framework with which we can explore the consequences of changing conditions in the labour market on the aggregate supply function, and the effects of changing the conditions of production on this function. Throughout the analysis in the main text we shall keep the basic shape of aggregate supply function as constructed in part (D) of Figure 4.4. Of course the actual price level in the economy is not simply generated in terms of this discussion of aggregate supply but would involve its interaction with the aggregate demand schedule as indicated by the model developed in the first part of this Appendix. In the text these interactions are also explored but the main point to make concerns the way 'supply--siders' are determined to hold $\bar{G}$ and $\bar{M}$ fixed in the aggregate demand function equation (1). To increase either $\bar{G}$ or $\bar{M}$ is to push the aggregate demand curve out to the right in part (D) of the diagrams.

Notes

   1.   Probably the clearest exposition of this can be found in the articles collected in Fink (ed) (1982). Supply-side economics is most closely associated with the economist Arthur B. Laffer who is credited with developing the seminal analytical tool of this group - the 'Laffer Curve' (Laffer 1979). This Laffer curve is further discussed in Chapter 6 in the UK context. For an assessment of the impact of SSE on President Reagan's initial 'Programme for Economic Recovery' see Fink (op cit) and Midland Bank (1981 and 1983).
   2.   These extreme supply-side positions are most forcefully put by the rather journalistic accounts of Wanniski (1978) and particularly Gilder (1981).
   3.   For a discussion of this particular mechanism in the UK context see McGee and Feige (1982). A more theoretical specification can be found in Frey and Pommertine (1984).
   4.   Some of these distinctions between Monetarism and Austrian economics are developed further in Bosanquet (1983). Recently a further 'Neo-Austrian' variant of Hayek's position has been developed in the context of monetary control debates by suggesting doing away with the 'legal tender' and 'unit of account' aspects of money (Greenfield and Yeager 1983).
   5.   In fact this would not be the case. Altering the position of the production function by increasing the capital stock would have an effect on the demand for labour schedule in section A of the diagrams - it would shift the demand curve for labour out and hence put upward pressures on the price of labour. For simplicity and convenience this complication is left out of the analysis.
   6.   For a discussion of this neo-Austrian approach to the central role of entrepreneurial curiosity see Dolan (1976), Rizzo (1979) and Kirtzner (1982).

References

Beesley, M. and Littlechild, S. (1983), 'Privatization: Principles, Problems and Priorities' Lloyds Bank Review No 149 July.
Bosanquet, N. (1983), After the New Right, Heinemann, London.
Dolan, E.G. (ed) (1976), The Foundation of Modern

Austrian Economics Sheed and Ward Inc., Kansas City.

Fink, R.H. (ed) (1982), Supply-Side Economics: A Critical Appraisal University Press of America, Maryland.

Frey, B.S., and Pommertine, W.R. (1984), 'The Hidden Economy: State and Prospects of Measurement' Review of Income and Wealth Vol 30 No.1 March, pp.1-24.

Gilder, G. (1981), Wealth and Poverty Basic Books, New York.

Greenfield, R.L., and Yeager, L.B. (1983), 'A Laissez-Faire Approach to Monetary Stability' Journal of Money Credit and Banking Vol 15 No.3 August, pp.302-315.

Harris, L. (1981), Monetary Theory McGraw Hill Book Company, New York.

Kirtzner, I.M. (ed) (1982), Methods, Processes and Austrian Economics D.C. Heath & Co., Massachusetts.

Laffer, A. (1979), 'An Equilibrium Rational Macro-economic Framework' in N.M. Kamrany and R.H. Day (eds) Economic Issues of the Eighties Johns Hopkins University Press, Balitimore, U.S.A., pp.44-57.

Levačić, R., and Rebmann, A. (1982), Macro-economics, Macmillan, London.

McGee, R.T., and Feige, E.L. (1982), 'The Unobserved Economy and the U.K. Laffer Curve' Journal of Economic Affairs Vol 13 No.1 October, pp.36-43.

Midland Bank (1981), 'President Reagan's Economic Policy' Midland Bank Review, Summer, pp.22-30

Midland Bank, (1983), 'Reaganomics - an Interim Assessment' Midland Bank Review, Summer/Autumn, pp.22-30.

Pryke, R. (1982), 'The Comparative Performance of Public and Private Enterprises' Fiscal Studies, Vol 3 No.2 July, pp.68-81.

Rizzo, M.J. (ed) (1979), Time, Uncertainty and Disequilibrium, Heath Lexington Books, D.C. Heath, Massachusetts.

Rousseaus, S. (1981-82), 'The Poverty of Wealth', Journal of Post Keynesian Economics Vol No.2 Winter, pp.192-213.

Say, J.B. (1834), A Treatise on Political Economy, London.

Spengler, J.J. (1945), 'The Physiocrats and Say's Law of Markets II' The Journal of Political Economy Vol L11, pp.317-347.

Thompson, G.F. (1984), 'The Rolling Back of the

State' in McLennan, G. et al (eds) State and
Society in Contemporary Britain, Basil
Blackwell, Oxford.
Tomlinson (1981), 'The Economics of Politics and
Public Expenditure: a critique' Economy and
Society Vol 10 No.4 November, pp.381-402.
Wanniski, J. (1978), The Way the World Works Basic
Books, New York.

Chapter 5

TRADE AND COMPETITION POLICY

1. INTRODUCTION

In this chapter we shall explore the way the Conservatives have approached trade and competition policy, narrowly conceived, over the period since their election in 1979. Clearly the Conservatives have made a good deal of their commitment in general terms to greater competition in the economy as the previous chapter pointed out. Here, we look more closely at exactly how this general commitment has manifested itself with respect to a number of rather specific areas.

Trade and competition policy has both a domestic and an international aspect. On the international front we look at the Conservatives' current attitude towards the main institutional bodies that regulate UK 'trade policy', namely the EEC and GATT. In addition some comment is made with respect to various initiatives associated with the Department of Trade and Industry (DTI) in connection with trade policy. On the domestic front we shall concentrate upon issues like the proposed 'privatization' of certain activities associated with the National Health Service and with the Social Security System. We shall also look at the manner of approach the government has adopted towards the Monopolies Commission and the Office of Fair Trading - these forming the usual focus for domestic 'competition policy' debates. In addition the government has ranged quite widely over other perhaps less focused areas and in this context their attitude towards the Stock Exchange and financial innovation, for instance, is discussed. As mentioned in Chapter 3, the Stock Exchange is going through a period of rapid transformation partly at the behest of the government itself.

Finally in this chapter the central and important question of the Conservatives' attitude towards the Trade Unions is raised in the context of the legislative activity they have initiated to 'reform' Trade Union practices. Thus the chapter ends with a discussion of institutional changes in connection with competition policy in the labour market. It reflects upon the notion of 'monopoly' as being the central problem in this and other areas and with the issue of incomes policies. The argument here is that despite a rhetoric against incomes policies in general, the Conservatives have ironically initiated a very active incomes policy of their own. All this presents a useful background to the discussions of taxation and personal incentives issues to be pursued in the following chapter.

2. TRADE POLICY IN THE INTERNATIONAL ARENA

It is well known that one of the major lacuna in 'competition policy' is associated with the international trading environment. Whilst governments may pursue all sorts of 'laissez - faire' or other competitively orientated policies on the domestic front, they have shown a great resistance to extend these into the international sphere. Protection of existing trading relationships by either protecting domestic producers via subsidies, erecting tariff barriers against imports, arranging quota restrictions or directly subsidizing exports have become the stock in trade of many a government. The temptation to acquiesce to protectionism, in one way or another have proved too strong for most governments to withstand whatever their political persuasion. A whole range of arguments have subsequently been mounted to justify the protectionist devices that have thereby been installed or agreed to. The question that the election of a Conservative government in 1979 posed was whether the UK economy would now see a decisive break with practices of previous 'interfering' governments on this score, and witness a radical attack on the structure of both formal and informal mechanisms of trade protection.

Commenting on this in 1983 two economists in the distinctly right of centre journal The World Economy, made the following points:

In spite of a rhetorical commitment to

'market-orientated' and 'supply-side' economic policy, the Thatcher Government, in the United Kingdom, could not be accused of lack of zeal when it comes to countering the 'threat' of competition from 'low-cost' and 'unfair' imports - as is evidenced by its approach to textiles, Spanish cars and Japanese goods in general. (Cable and Weale 1983 p.421).

Here, then, is a familiar theme; the difference between what the Government says it will do and what has actually transpired. The more overtly Right wing Adam Smith Institute re-inforces this view when commenting upon what it sees as the inward looking and protectionist shift that the EEC took during the 1970s:

The present Conservative government has done little or nothing to reverse the direction of Britain's influence: and indeed when new issues have arisen - the renegotiation of the MFA (Multi-Fibre Agreement) and recent conflicts with Japan, for example - it has tended to continue in the same direction. In effect, its contribution has been to allow things to get worse more slowly. (Adam Smith Institute 1984a p.26)

It goes on to suggest that this is because of a 'lack of courage' on the part of the Conservatives, thereby rendering their position into a matter of 'will power'.

Clearly, this is not a sufficient form of analysis (as the Institute in fact recognises) since the UK economy is caught in a system of constraints with respect to what it can and cannot do on the international trade front. The bulk of Britain's trade policy is predetermined by membership of the EEC and GATT. It does not have real control over important instruments of policy like tariffs or over policy in key sectors like agriculture, textiles and clothing, or steel. Domestic agricultural trade policy is largely controlled through the Common Agricultural Policy of the EEC in which Margaret Thatcher has been a key figure in trying to reform along not unreasonable lines (though she has tended to go about this in quite an unreasonable manner - see Appendix 1). The trade in textiles and clothing is highly regulated on a worldwide basis via the Multi-fibre Agreement (MFA) established in 1973 and recently re-newed under the Conservatives in 1981 (Keesing and Wolf 1981). The European Community's steel industry and trade in steel is protected in the form of an official cartel designed to rationalize European steel production over an acceptable period of time. This was established in 1977 in the face of decline in the market for steel and the 'dumping' of cheap steel into the community from a range of third party countries including the Eastern Europeans, the USA, Japan and some of the LDCs. It is due to end in 1985.

In fact, apart from these areas, the UK is not a highly protected economy in terms of tariff barriers on traded goods. Seven successful rounds of GATT negotiations since its inception in 1947 aimed at reducing tariffs have resulted in an estimated weighted average tariff on industrial products of only 4.7% around the community as a whole. Intra-community trade is subject to zero tariffs, as is Britain's trade with EFTA countries. Tariff barriers are, then not a major issue in debates about 'trade policy' apart from the MFA and steel production, to which I return below.

However, there are some other areas of major dispute and argument. These concern non-tariff barriers broadly speaking, particularly so called 'voluntary restraint agreements' (VRAs), and subsidies to home producers of various forms. In addition the problem of trade barriers in the field of services is becoming a major issue.

Like any system of regulation the GATT framework includes a number of somewhat vague statutes which allow a range of interpretations and hence enable an undermining of its original intentions. This also sets up incentives to circumvent the framework itself. There are always unresolved tensions and contradictions written into any regulatory procedure. Article XIX of GATT is one such example. This is meant to regulate protection against a sudden surge of imports of a particular product. It can be interpreted to authorise 'emergency protection', but only if this is 'non-discriminatory' and genuinely 'voluntary'. Largely to avoid these latter two aspects and so as to be freer to interpret what might constitute a 'serious injury' to domestic industry, some countries - particularly the highly industrialized ones - have resorted to the development of VRAs when their industry has been 'threatened'. These operate to restrict the volume of exports coming from foreign countries. They are in effect imports quota arranged on a bilateral basis. Such VRAs have proliferated during the post-1973 period. Products covered by such restraints in the UK include footwear (with South Korea, Taiwan, Czechoslovakia, Poland and Romania), pottery (with Japan and Taiwan), cutlery (with Japan, South Korea, and Taiwan), colour television sets (with Japan), portable monochrome television sets (with Japan, Singapore, South Korea and Taiwan), monochrome television sets (with Japan) and cars (with Japan) (Jones 1983). Other European Community members particularly France, are also active in these areas but increasingly it is the Community itself which is conducting the negotiations. Here Japan is seen as the main problem. Early in 1983 the Japanese agreed to operate quantitative trade restraints on the export of videotape recorders to the Community not to exceed 4.55 millions in 1983 (with similar restrictions for the following two years) and also to limit their exports of colour TV sets to 900,000 in 1983. They further agreed to monitor their exports of a wide range of other goods including light commercial vehicles, forklift trucks, motorcycles, quartz watches, hi-fi equipment, cars and numerically controlled machine tools - on which the Commission had originally sought quantitative restrictions.

The question that arises in connection with this discussion of VRAs is their probable economic effects. Those committed to a market orientated approach to economic policy are thrown into a veritable frenzy by these kinds of restrictions, condemning them out of hand. However, to put this into its proper perspective it is estimated by GATT that only about 5% of total world trade was affected in the early 1980s. VRAs affect about 8% of US trade and probably between 7 to 10% of UK trade (reported in Hindley 1980 p.316). They tend, however, to be concentrated within particular industries as we have seen above, where their impact might be more significant. But by any means 'distortions' caused by VRAs are as yet unlikely to be of major economic importance.

Cartelization is likely to be one of the responses to the negotiation of a VRA in the exporting country. When a quota is agreed some mechanism must be sought to allocate this between the various producers within the exporting country concerned. Any quota holder in effect has a guaranteed market, and usually a guaranteed price as well. This can lead to all sorts of well known undesirable economic effects.

It can also have a range of problematical affects in the importing country, though these are not always easy to discern and fully quantify. Orthodox economic trade theory is not a particularly useful tool under these circumstances since it is still predominantly set in terms of perfect competition. In practice we are dealing with oligopoly and collusion. Under these circumstances Dixit has recently pointed to a possible consequence:

> Consider a duopoly where the home and foreign firms are unable to sustain collusion by themselves. Now let the home government impose an import quota. This makes it profitable for the home firm to raise the price somewhat, with the assurance that the foreign firm will not be able to sell more by undercutting. Then the foreign firm can sell its quota amount at a higher price. This can increase both firms' profits. The effect of the quota is to allow collusion, i.e. it is a facilitating practice. (Dixit 1984 p.6).

This is an important point. An import quota might stimulate tacit collusion between home and foreign country producers unless other measures are instituted to monitor this and prevent it happening. Such a situation would obviously affect consumer welfare in the home country and this has been much stressed by free-market commentators. But such a conclusion depends crucially upon what other compensating factors might arise within the domestic economy. The maintenance of jobs is important for instance and could compensate for some loss of consumer welfare. While the TUC in the UK stresses this aspect of things, arguing for protection to 'core' industries to enable any necessary structural re-adustment to take place over an acceptable period of time (eg TUC 1984 with respect to the MFA), the CBI has also advocated import restrictions for instances where competition is 'unfair' and where the speed of adjustment would be otherwise too rapid.

Some method of assessing the likely net impact of import restrictions is required when all the interdependent and conpensation adjustments in the home economy have had a chance to work themselves through. A recent study has tried to do just this with respect to two sectors - textiles and

clothing, and motor vehicles. Using the Cambridge
Economic Growth Model - a large multi-sectoral,
input output based macro-economic model of the UK
economy - Cable and Weale (1983) tried to assess
the overall economic consequences of holding the
import penetration in the two areas constant at
1980 levels. To do this they had to assume away the
problem mentioned above, i.e. that either home or
foreign producers would act to raise their prices
and increase their profit margins.

The results of this kind of analysis enable
differences between the 'national interest' and
sectoral, or sectional interests to be highlighted.
While those involved in the immediate industry
concerned may gain, the wider community might
suffer some loss of welfare in terms of overall
personal disposable income. This is exactly how
things turned out and there were also variations in
effects as between the two sectors. By and large a
significant overall net loss resulted in the
textile and clothing case, while a more even
position emerged in the motor vehicles case. In
terms of the instruments of protection employed to
produce the desired objective, the erection of
tariff barriers was considered the least efficient,
the extension of quotas the next least efficient,
while a real depreciation of the currency plus
downward pressure on labour costs seemed the most
acceptable way of reducing imports and encouraging
exports.

Clearly more needs to be done in terms of
these disaggregated sectoral analysis before the
pros and cons of particular forms of economic
protection can be judged. An outright condemnation
is as equally unsatisfactory as a call for general
and comprehensive import quotas on all traded goods
and services.

It is difficult to discern exactly what the
Thatcher Government's policy is on many of these
issues. It certainly has not gone for a full scale
and radical dismantling of existing trade barriers.
If anything it has cautiously encouraged and
supported the status quo. Like its predecessors and
like most other industrialized countries, it has
adopted a very pragmatic approach. The champion of
the 'consumer interest' has not as yet gone over
the heads of either the EEC, the CBI or the TUC.
Working within the context of the European
Community the Government has allowed additional
restrictions where these could be negotiated easily
with exporters (VRAs) or where the exporters

retaliatory capacity was weak (many of the LDCs).
It has also accepted protectionist positions where
imports were thought to constitute 'unfair'
competition because they were being dumped (Eastern
Europe mainly), where trade is bilaterally
unbalanced (as in the case of Japan) or where the
exporting country maintains significant protective
barriers itself (eg. Brazil, Korea and Spain).
There seems little reason to expect things to
change much on this score in the near future.
Though this may change with respect to the
particular case of the MFA, since the DTI has
launched an investigation into the effects of this
on the UK economy prior to its renegotiation in a
year or two's time. Any such change in stance would
have to be negotiated in an international context
however.

We can now look more closely at the other two
areas mentioned above where significant non-tariff
barriers present contentious issues. Industrial
subsidization is one such area. While import
controls and voluntary restraint operate on foreign
supplies, industrial subsidies either act as a
barrier to imports or as a subsidy to exporters.
Such subsidies can be very effective instruments
for individual governments to conduct their trade
policies. A wide range of industries in the UK are
protected in this way - steel, vehicles, shipbuilding,
aero-engines, aircraft, nuclear power and others.
Clearly these are not just subsidized for
international trade reasons but also in the context
of domestic orientated policies. The Community
itself also conducts such subsidy policies vis-a-
vis steel and agriculture in particular. The
estimated costs of these subsidies are significant
- £2.8 billions in 1980 for the Common Agricultural
Policy paid by UK consumers, £1.4 billions for
restriction on car imports, £0.5 billions for
tariffs and quotas on textiles and clothes. All in
all approximately £4 billions overall for the UK as
a whole (quoted in Adam Smith Institute 1984 p.25).
These figures might be exaggerated but they
probably indicate the broad levels involved.

Mrs Thatcher's attempt to reform the Common
Agricultural Policy could have some effect on the
sums involved, but it is unlikely that a massive
reduction in agricultural support overall will
ensue. As mentioned in Chapter 2 it is more likely
that such support will simply be thrown back onto
domestic expenditure, rather than eliminated
altogether. The Conservatives have never been

strong proponents of eliminating agricultural price support as a whole. In the other two main areas mentioned above the Conservatives have either been instrumental in establishing the quotas (cars) or in agreeing to their continuation (MFA). Reducing subsidies to the nationalized industry sector, which is the other main area of subsidization to manufacturing activity is one of their major concerns. This is further reviewed in Chapter 7 and their prospects here are uncertain.

On the question of services and their protection even less has been achieved by the Conservatives. The GATT framework is not so important here as it has proved more difficult to establish an effective initiative within this organization to investigate and then 'reform' service sector trading arrangements (Schott 1983). From the point of view of the UK economy, the EEC is a much more important forum. 'Harmonization' of various kinds is proceeding within the Community but very slowly and with respect to a rather limited set of issues.

Services are not subject to the traditional kinds of trade restrictions (tariffs, quotas etc) but are subject to barriers made manifest in administrative forms. They are also complex and heterogeneous in character which makes it difficult to establish a simple or comprehensive set of principles and rules by which they could be regulated internationally. As a result piecemeal negotiation and agreement would seem more or less inevitable.

The establishment and provision of services like banking, insurance, transport and travel, information data gathering and communication etc., continue to be closely regulated on a national basis, purportedly to safeguard the domestic public against financial and other risks. There can be little doubt that these kinds of regulations involve statutory and administrative practices which systematically discriminate against companies solely on their basis of residency or ownership. It is this later aspect that those arguing for less interference with the free flow of services among countries wish to see tackled in an international context. With the growing interdependence of national service markets this task probably becomes more pressing. While the US has taken a lead in arguing along these lines and the UK has followed in the European context, little has been achieved. This is even more the case in a range of professional services as with medical or para-medical activities, architects, legal advisors etc.

It is not difficult to see why the USA and to a lesser extent the UK should want to push for the liberalization of trade in services faster than some of the other advanced industrialized countries. They have a comparative advantage in these areas. The UK is particularly interested in liberalizing the trade in financial services since it sees London as the 'natural' European base for these, given its already highly developed status as a financial centre. All this must probably await the tortuous 'harmonization' agreement negotiations with respect to taxation matters, company disclosure requirements, accountancy conventions, legal services etc., which are under way within the EEC. These negotiations would be a constraint on any UK Government however committed it might be to 'liberalization' and 'de-regulation' in these areas. Alternatively, with respect to financial services, the normal competitive framework associated with the increasingly interdependent financial and money markets, could (and probably will) lead to an increasing breakdown of any remaining 'artificial' barriers to their working at the domestic level. This is likely to be the case almost despite the stance adopted by domestic governments. In a sense, then, the rapidly developing financial innovation in these already highly internationalized markets (already raised in Chapter 3), have rendered a good deal of domestic regulation virtually redundant and unworkable. It could be argued that the problem is less one of 'leading' with a policy for the liberalization of service barriers, but more one of gaining some kind of control or leverage on such markets themselves which are rapidly developing their own independent momentum. Meaningful policy responses in this area are seriously needed, and proving difficult to come by in the framework of international negotiations. This was pointed out in Chapter 3 when dealing with Latin American and other countries' debt rescheduling problems.

In this area and in the others just mentioned, the Conservatives have more or less followed the same stance as their predecessors in government. They all seem to have lacked a coherent trade policy - it being made up of a series of rather ad hoc compromises dictated by political expectancy in the main. In relationship to the Common Market this is probably how things will remain. Indeed a recent Centre for Policy Studies booklet, dealing

with the Conservative Party's policy towards the
Community, underlined the following statement as
its basic position. We believe the way forward lies
in pragmatic, piecemeal measures, improving,
adapting and, where appropriate, extending the
European Community we have (Centre for Policy
Studies 1984 p.7). The detailed policy suggestions
contained in the document follow this line to the
letter. All in all the Government has been almost
ultra-cautious with respect to trade policy, not
seeming to wish to upset any party or any
established mechanism of trade regulation. At home,
it has been somewhat more active however -
subsidies to industry and particularly the
nationalized ones are to be cut, the DTI is to be
re-modelled to act as the spearhead of a renewed
aggressive approach to international competition
with the private sector in the forefront. In this
latter context initiatives are likely to be made in
the near future with respect to the Export Credits
Guarantee Department. In April 1984 a report
commissioned by the DTI suggested this should be
turned into a public corporation - enabling it to
borrow from the private financial markets and
reinsure some risks with the private sector. An
additional idea here was to reduce the capacity of
this privatized body to subsidise UK exports - one
of the main advantages seen to emanate from such a
change in the ECGD status. Ironically perhaps these
'advantages' claimed for a new semi-privatized ECGD
along these lines appeared in the Financial Times
directly alongside a report about how Metro-Cammell,
the British urban railcar builder, had just lost a
contract to supply Singapore's Underground system.
The $280 million contract was won by the Japanese
in the face of fierce international competition.

> A key advantage was in organizing finance. The
> Singapore Chinese as a whole tend to put a
> large weight on price in such matters, and the
> Japanese had the greatest flexibility because
> of the versatility of Mitsui, the large
> trading house acting as their agent in
> Singapore. For example the Japanese could
> offer Singapore a fixed foreign exchange rate
> up to 1990 at no extra cost. British industry,
> Government and financial institutions are not
> geared up to provide that kind of guarantee.
> (Financial Times April 12th 1984 p.26).

The Japanese saw this project as having long

119

term strategic consequences in terms of their breaking into a new market and they adjusted their 'subsidy' accordingly. It could thus be said with some justification that while the Government was 'fiddling' in the UK, Metro-Cammell, with just a single and by all accounts exhausted negotiator in Singapore, was 'burning'. According to the Financial Times' own report, with the loss of this contract probably went the prospects of supplying other rapid transit systems in the future.

In fact the prospects of privatizing the ECGD rather faded in mid 1984 when it was announced that little interest could be found from among the private financial interests for 'buying into' it.

3.   COMPETITION POLICY IN THE DOMESTIC ARENA

Although the EEC has its own framework of competition policy - to scrutinize intra Community mergers and restrictive trade practices - its apparatus is still relatively underdeveloped compared to trusted and tried national institutional mechanisms. In the UK this is organised under the Office of Fair Trading via the Restrictive Practices Court and the Monopolies and Mergers Commission.

This official framework is supplemented by an 'unofficial' City Takeover Panel, which acts on behalf of City institutions and the Stock Exchange in scrutinizing possible mergers. The Monopolies Commission was created by the Monopoly and Restrictive Practices Act of 1948 while the Restrictive Practices Court was created eight years later in 1956. It is the various 'public interest' criteria by which the Monopolies Commission has judged the efficiency of proposed takeovers and mergers since 1973, that has caused most controversy. The main Conservative legislative initiative in respect to this area was embodied in the 1980 Competition Act. This exhorted the Director General of Fair Trading to carry out an investigation where it appeared to him that any person has been or is following a course of conduct which may amount to an anti-competitive practice. Such an anti-competitive practice is defined by the Act as:

A course of conduct pursued by a person in the course of business, which has, or is intended to have, or is likely to have, the effect of restricting, distorting or preventing competition

120

in connection with the production, supply or acquisition of goods in the UK, or any part of it on the supply or security of services in the UK or any part of it.

As should be apparent this is a very vague criteria - so that what constitutes the 'public interest' with respect to it is difficult to discern. This has been seized upon by Right wing critics of the legislation to try to discredit the work of the Monopolies Commission in particular arguing that its work simply gives licence to bureaucratic and administrative control over something which should be left to normal commercial practice to establish.

In fact a major Green Paper of 1978 (HMSO 1978) - the Liesner Report - proposed a 'neutral' policy towards takeovers in place of the 'benign' approach embodied in existing legislation. Any proposed merger is condemned only if it is found likely to work against the public interest. The Liesner proposals would have required the demonstration of positive effects and benefits, but this approach was not followed up in the 1980 Act in order to strengthen the Monopolies Commission. By contrast it preserved at least the spirit of the traditional view by only allowing investigations into what are termed 'anti-competitive practices' as defined above and thereby addressed restrictive trade practices only.

Only large mergers can be referred to the Monopolies Commission involving assets to be taken over of more than £15 million, or mergers where a share of the relevant market of 25% or more would be created or enhanced. The most important body in merger policy is in fact the Merger Panel (Kay and Silberston 1984). This is a committee of civil servants and Office of Fair Trading staff which recommends whether a merger should be referred. Lobbying in respect to this panel against a potential reference, or for it where a reluctant party is involved (since they expect an unfavourable judgement on mergers) has become the most important stage in the whole procedure. Very few eligible mergers are ever referred to the Commission. Most are cleared by the Merger Panel. It is at the Merger Panel stage that government policy towards take-over activity becomes important and is made manifest. Since the 1980 Act the government has indicated that it wishes to re-emphasise the benign approach - i.e. that it will only act on recommendations if mergers are thought to work negatively against the public interest. Ministerial statements have suggested a more sceptical approach towards mergers should be adopted - particularly with respect to conglomerate or diversification mergers - although nothing 'sinister' is thought to necessarily emanate from these. But some confusion in all of this emerged in 1982 when the recommendation of the Monopolies Commission not to allow the proposed merger between Charter Consolidated and Anderson Strathclyde was reversed by the Minister of Trade. In addition in 1983 the then Minister Mr Cecil Parkinson rejected the Director General of Fair Trading's recommendation that the acquisition of Rank Hovis/McDougall's agricultural service by Dalgety should be referred to the Commission. Thus great uncertainty has arisen about what criteria are to be applied with respect to mergers and on what basis judgements are to be made. In connection to this the DTI set up a review group on these criteria which promised to report in the Autumn of 1984. What is clear, however, is that this Conservative government is no more radically committed <u>against</u> private 'monopolization' than any of its predecessors. 'Competition policy' in the UK has not prevented it from becoming one of the most 'concentrated' industrial structures amongst advanced nations, and this is unlikely to change under the Conservatives.

However, the Conservatives have pushed the scope of their competition policy and restrictive practice legislation into the purview of the Public Corporations. They have also opened up minor areas like opticians to competition by allowing more or less anyone to provide spectacles if they wish and if they can meet minimal safeguards. Nothing of a more fundamental nature with respect to merger legislation is likely to follow, however, despite the relative failure of the 1980 Competition Act and the subsequent uncertainty about precise criteria of referral and judgement to the Monopolies Commission. The Commission will continue to be viewed as a fairly weak body, adding ammunition to those sniping at it from the Right of the Conservatives. It is interesting to note that these critics are on the one hand fond of quoting the famous line from Adam Smith about how businessmen seldom get together without this leading to some conspiracy against the public, or contrivance to raise prices, while on the other they wish to dismantle one of the very instruments designed to prevent this happening.

A further important development under the Conservatives with respect to 'competition policy' concerns their attitude towards the Stock Exchange. The Restrictive Trade Practices (Stock Exchange) Bill, passed in 1983, represented a response by the Conservative to the Office of Fair Trading's proposed investigations (under the 1980 Act) into the restrictive, or 'anti-competitive' practices of the Exchange. In particular, for an agreement by the Stock Exchange to abandon its practices of minimum commissions on share dealings, the Act exempted it from the scope of the restrictive practices legislation altogether.

Although the Act only instituted a rather gentle three year adjustment period in which the distinction between jobbers and brokers was to be eliminated and some outsiders were to be let into the market, it heralded a massive and rapid shake up in Stock Exchange practices. These far outran initial expectations. Suddenly a near free for all with respect to outside interest in Stock Exchange dealings was initiated, with stock-broker firms being first courted and then rapidly merged both with UK merchant banks and commercial banks. American banks were also quite heavily involved.

Meanwhile The Stock Exchange, with the active co-operation of the Bank of England, initiated a wide ranging review of how it might be supervised and regulated in the future, and into exactly what character its reformulated commercial practices should take. This is being pushed along by the rapid changes in ownership and organization, involving the newly amalgamating stock jobbing and stock broking business.

Behind this somewhat frenetic activity of the later 1983 early 1984 period lie deeper economic reasons. The name of the financial game in the mid 1980s looks likely to be 'financial conglomeration'. The growing interdependences of financial markets on a global scale already referred to in Chapter 3, is the real force pushing these organizational changes in which banks and stock broker firms are amalgamating. British firms already have stakes in Far Eastern markets and new American liaisons are quickly developing. This will help establish truly international and integrated financial houses at the wholesale end of the financial spectrum, based in the UK, which it is hoped will be able to compete effectively with already existing American firms. The banks look set to become the dominant partners in this relationship since it is they who can provide the capital base for such operations and who have the financial muscle to carry it off.

Interestingly enough these tendencies at the wholesale and international level are being paralled somewhat at the retail and national level. Here again financial conglomeration and diversification are developing. While fifteen years ago the dominant idea in UK financial circles was specialization now it is towards the integration of a wide range of financial services within a single organizational entity. This is being pushed particularly by the Building Societies. These innovating institutions - rapidly transforming themselves into ordinary commercial banks in all but name - have argued that they should be able to conduct genuine retail and even wholesale banking business in competition with the clearing banks. These tendencies were given institutional backing when the Conservatives issued a Green Paper in July 1984 which proposed to grant Building Societies powers for full money transmission services. In addition conveyancing and structural surveying activity, associated with house sale and purchase would be granted to them (HMSO 1984). Meanwhile the banks have delved into the mortgage market, even if with some trepidation. Competition between the two organizations in both forms of finance and dealing is likely to develop in the future as the Societies are gradually integrated into the formal banking structure. The scenario is for both of these to develop into integrated financial service institutions in which customers would be offered banking, mortgage, conveyancing services, insurance, other financial services and even estate agency and travel booking facilities all under one roof. Whether this will be allowed to fully develop, or how soon, is open to dispute but in the name of greater competition the Conservatives have not shown themselves adverse to those possible developments (although the Bank of England is more cautious, since it would have to supervise this structure).

What the Conservatives have shown themselves positively in favour of is the opening up of the Stock Exchange to the kinds of 'competitive forces' described above. However, the obvious retort here is to question the logic of developing international financial conglomerates in the name of competition. Once again a real contradiction emerges in this context. Competition is justified in terms of a

process which actually involves the concentration
of capital. This raises an important theoretical
question what is meant by competition? The
Conservatives would seem to justify this in terms
of a kind of 'Neo-Austrian' approach. In this
context the issue is less one of the _size_ of
capital involved, relative to some appropriate
measure of the extent of the market, but more one
of the _potential_ for entry into that market.
'Competition' is thus seen in terms of a kind of
market 'process' in which the size of the
organizations within it are of secondary importance
to the capacity of some agent to enter the market
if 'monopoly power' there leads to an economic
inefficiency. The Conservatives idea of a competitive
market structure is not thus a neo-classical one,
but is seen more in terms of Baumol's (1982)
'contestable markets' thesis. As long as 'barriers
to entry' are kept low by state action and the
market can be potentially contested, all will be
well. Some have even developed a slightly different
attack along these lines to argue that any
'monopoly profits' arising in the context of large
organizations are almost a positive feature of the
market process. They signal a premium for taking
risks and innovating (Littlechild 1981). In the
longer term they will be bid away by other
innovating entrepreneurs. This is in fact a rather
classical Shumpeterian rationalization for the
'short-term' existence of monopoly profits.

4.   'PRIVATIZING' THE SOCIAL SERVICES AND THE
      NATIONAL HEALTH SERVICE

The supposed attack on 'anti-competitive practices'
has not been confined to the private sector.
Arguments and policy have also been directed
towards public activity as well. As mentioned above
the 1980 Competition Act allowed the Office of Fair
Trading to investigate the nationalized industries
and refer them to the Monopolies Commission.
     But alongside this have developed some direct
initiatives to change the character of the social
services particularly the Health Service's pension
arrangements. The background to this is the
dramatic rise in social services expenditure as a
proportion of overall government expenditure. The
NHS and certain parts of the social services have
been picked out as possible sources of savings.
This would also have the 'merit', it is argued, of

increasing competition in these areas.In June 1984 Professor Patrick Minford of Liverpool University published a set of proposals designed to dismantle the welfare state and re-organize it under private provision. On pensions he suggests:

> The Ultimate object is to transfer all pensions, including basic state pension, into private schemes financed by private contributions...... I envisage that the State will allow any institution, profit making or non-profiting making which is licenced to offer pensions, to provide the state minimum package either on its own or as a part of a bigger package. Market competition will ensure the best terms for individual buyers. (Minford 1984 p. X).

On the Health Service he writes:

> The Ultimate objective here is to have everyone covered by a minimum standard of 'comprehensive' (private) health insurance .... With everyone insured in this way and paying cash for treatment by doctors in hospitals, health provision would be privatized, but in such a way as to create competition in each geographic area (p.XI).

On education he writes:

> .....the objective is to have everyone pay for their own school and university fees, and to make primary and secondary education compulsory as now. At the same time we wish to have education service competitively provided in the private sector...... To ensure competition no one educational 'firm' could own more than one of the schools in any catchment area (p.XII).

There are similar proposals for other areas like personal social services and various social benefits but these are taken up in the following chapter under a discussion of the 'negative income tax' proposals.

All in all Minford suggests that these kinds of radical changes, plus a range of others associated with public provision of goods and services, could save the state some £43 billion a year by 1990. The publication of this report virtually coincided with the announcement that the Social Services Secretary Mr Norman Fowler was initiating an extensive long term review of Social Services provision (though he also stressed that this did not necessarily imply the objective was to deliberately cut back on expenditure in these areas).

Minford's paper has the merit (perhaps dubious merit?) of bringing together a typical set of proposals that have been increasingly vocally, advocated by the 'New Right' with respect to welfare expenditure over the early 1980s period. The intention here is not to develop a thorough going critique of these principles but simply to pick out a couple of areas and look more closely into what has gone on in terms of the government's actual practice in these areas, and what some of the constraints on future developments might be.

First it will be useful to draw a distinction between liberalization, privatization and de-nationali-zation. By liberalization is meant a process in which greater potential competition is opened up in an area by the State either de-regulating certain economic activities or changing the statutory conditions under which they can operate. Such is the case with areas like transport provision, the Stock Exchange discussed above, or the provision of spectacles and the like as also discussed above. This process does not in itself change ownership conditions - any state owned bodies could still be involved as _one_ of the parties in the provision process. De-nationalization on the other hand involves a process of the widespread sale of the productive assets of a large area of economic activity previously owned and operated exclusively by a State agency. This is discussed in Chapter 7. By 'privatization' is meant the 'letting out', franchising, or tendering of a particular limited service by the state or one of its agencies to private contractors, which was previously exclusive, provided by that state or governmental body itself. Ownership rights are not directly involved here.

Up until now it has been this kind of 'privatization' that has typified the Social Welfare and Health Service provision activities. Elements of these, like school meals provision, rubbish collection and disposal, catering and cleaning in the Health Service, etc., are now operated by private contractors - and this kind of essentially ad-hoc 'privatization' is likely to continue in the future. Indeed it is nothing new.

127

It has a long tradition within some of the National- ized Industries. For instance the British Airports Authority franchises car parking and other commercial activities at their airports. British Rail also franchise rail terminal commercial activity. In principle there seems nothing objectionable to this, other than when it is deliberately done to force wages down, as has sometimes been the case with school meal provision and National Health Service cleaning services in recent years. The terms of this 'privatization' activity is what should be at stake.

Let us now look at an example of what has actually happened in the provision of Social Security Benefits - namely the National Insurance Sickness Benefit (NISB). The government issued a Green Paper in April 1980 outlining a series of possible changes in this scheme to throw some of the expenditure on sickness pay and benefits back on to employers and employees (HMSO 1980). Subsequently a modified variant of one of the schemes outlined in the Green Paper became effective in April 1983. This is the only piece of welfare 'privatization' enacted so far. Michael O'Higgins has carefully charted the course of this initiative in a series of recent articles (O'Higgins 1981, 1983 and 1984). As yet it is difficult to judge exactly what overall effects the scheme is likely to have. The intention was to require employers to pay a flat rate sick pay to their employees for the first eight weeks in any one year. In fact with this move some 90% of benefit claims would thereby be covered. The employers would be compensated by a reduction in their national insurance contribution liability. It was argued that this would compensate the employers for the extra cost, allowing a projected reduction in public expenditure of £375 million at the expense of a loss of £420 million in national insurance contributions. However, the new statutory sickness pay would be liable to income tax and national insurance contributions. This would produce a projected income of £200 million to the Inland Revenue and the Government expected a further savings in administration costs of some £30 million. Overall then public expenditure would fall by some £400 million, for a net revenue loss of only £200 million.

One problem identified by O'Higgins with the finally adopted scheme, was that its flat rate character discriminates against single-wage couples

128

and those with children. It also discriminates against the low paid who receive lower flat rates commensurate with their lower wages while in work. He suggested, however, that collective bargaining might counteract some of these effects (O'Higgins 1984 p.134).

In the event the government was forced to give more generous compensation to employers to get them to co-operate with the scheme than it had first bargained for. Compensation worth £565m was offered to reduce public spending by £400m. This increase in compensation absorbed much of the revenue gains from taxing sick pay, so that the net gain to the PSBR was only £40m instead of the expected £200m. The practical effect of this is that the taxation of statutory sick pay has funded an income transfer from employees to employers! (1984 p.135). But not a very large one, it might be added.

O'Higgins also points out that once the practice of occupationally based benefits systems have been established, with appropriate state regulation (as opposed to 'provision'), arguments can begin to be mounted for their extension and widening. Manual workers can bargain for similar benefits as their better provided for non-manual colleagues and women can argue for similar treatment as men. Thus equality may be increased, and recent German experience, where a similar scheme operates, suggests that it actually has been increased, he argues (O'Higgins 1981 p.155).

When reviewing the Conservatives' approach to the provision of social welfare benefits in more general terms, it is pointed out that despite planned cuts, actual real expenditure has increased dramatically. The emphasis shifted in 1982, however, to cash planning and away from service provision planning. Unemployment and other benefits also become subject to taxation, and means tested benefits increased at the expense of non-discriminatory benefits. All in all the effects of this have been to reduce the rate of spending growth from four times to three times that planned under the last Labour administration (O'Higgins 1983 p.170).

What are the reasons for this failure of the Conservatives to cut-back on welfare expenditure? O'Higgins suggests that this:

......is a result neither of its falling prey to the centrist seductions of Whitehall nor of previously unreported victories by Conservative wets, but by the dissonance between the rhetoric of cuts and the reality of the political and economic role of public spending in a complex industrial society (O'Higgins 1983 p.154).

In particular spending on income maintenance - accounting for over a quarter of all public expenditure - is not subject to cash limits because it is demand determined. It is dependent upon how many people claim their statutory rights with respect to such benefits and this is outside of the immediate control of the government. In addition the political power and influence of the elderly is not to be dismissed as a reason for the climb down of Mrs Thatcher in trying to cut-back on the real value of pensions. The maintenance of the real value of these and of child benefits and of disability pensions, at least up until the Autumn of 1984, was also linked to the pressure from Conservative backbenchers who have consistently pushed for the effective index-linking of these benefits. Since then there has been some erosion of real benefit levels.

What are the prospects for the future with respect to welfare 'privatization' and cut-backs in expenditure? Unless the Government is seriously to break the 'welfare consensus' and begin to dismantle the welfare state along Minford type lines, the realistic options look extremely limited. There would certainly be intense and widespread political resistance to this, not least from within the Conservative Party itself. In a sense the Conservatives have worked themselves into a contradictory position. They argue that the recession, with, its high levels of unemployment and reductions in real wages, is a necessary if unfortunate feature of the requirement to revitalize the economy. Along with this must go a reduction in public expenditure to keep inflationary pressures under control and enable the private sector to flourish. But these two aspects are not compatible since the former results in an increase in expenditure on unemployment benefit provision and other income maintenance programmes. An aging population, recent increases in the birth rate and the likelihood of increased unemployment make this contradiction look even worse for the future. But these latter tendencies would have to be coped with by any government committed to the preservation of a welfare state in the form in which it has developed over the Post-War period. They present real long-term structural problems which will require long-term policy responses. The Conservatives are in no different position with respect to this than would be governments of other political persuasions, though they may try to go about tackling it in their own particular style. What is clear is that a scheme to let all this be conveniently taken care of by the 'market mechanism' is as unlikely to succeed as one which simply defends all the existing range, scale and forms of the present welfare state. This should become clearer as we look at another area of a welfare provision in slightly more detail - namely the NHS.

There has been considerable disquiet shown about the possible break-up of the NHS. Around the time of the 1983 General Election widespread accusations and denials circulated about the Conservatives' real intentions and attitude towards the health service. Its 'privatization' at the earliest possible moment was rumoured. The spectre of an American style health system was raised and constant reminders of the growth of private medicine in the UK referred to. In mid 1984 the Right wing pressure group The Adam Smith Institute published a report echoing Minford's proposals as outlined above. It called for charges to be instituted for a wide range of health services including 'hotel style' services like hospital bed linen and food, for Family Planning Services, visits to GPs, for the use of ambulances and drugs. All these would be means tested and subject to compulsory private insurance (Adam Smith Institute 1984b).

But let us put some of this into perspective. For instance in 1980 some 94% of total expenditure on health services was undertaken by the NHS (a higher percentage than in Sweden) and of the remaining 'private' 6%, half of this was for over the counter medicines bought at chemists, supermarkets and the like. Private hospitals accounted for only 2.6% of expenditure. In real terms private health spending rose by <u>less</u> than public spending over the period 1970-80, though there was an increase in the proportion of <u>private capital</u> spending within these trends.

As one commentator has put it:

> .....the private sector is best at repairing hernias and replacing varicose veins......its range of activities is very narrow: about 30

> procedures account for 60 per cent of
> expenditure.....there is no scientific evidence
> that it is more efficient than the NHS......
> (Maynard 1983 p.38).

The bulk of day to day health care activity and large scale or emergency surgery is still carried out within the NHS - even for those covered by private health care schemes. The development of private health insurance is hampered by a number of things, not least the stagnant condition of the economy. This puts constraints on the private sector development as well as on the public sector. Recruitment to these schemes from amongst trade unionists is static, for instance. Growth rates for recruitment more generally were only 3% in 1982 and 2% in 1983 while private hospital charges trebled between 1978 and 1983. Health care premiums were rising at a rate of 25% per year.

But perhaps the main constraint on these developments can be illustrated by looking at Table 5.1 where the per-capita cost of health care is given for a number of age ranges. The private schemes have recruited from the 'healthy' section of the community - roughly those of working age (15-64 years). These happen also to co-incide with the ages at which health care costs are the lowest. It is with the very young and the very old that health costs escalate, up to 6 or 7 times that of working age people. Private schemes are unlikely to be able to cope with these kinds of expenditures and nor would a government be likely to allow a 'contracting out' of its healthy population so that it is left with supporting just the young and the very old. If nothing else an aging population puts a massive constraint on the development of private health schemes in the UK context.

In addition, US experience shows that to hand over medicine to private organization also effectively means a handover of medicine to the control of doctors. The role of doctors' influence in resources allocation can be quite undesirable, even within the context of the NHS. It has led to the concentration of spending in prestige areas such as teaching hospitals, major surgery, fundamental research, etc. This is ever more the case in the USA. There the private provision of medicine has led to a more expensive, 'surgery intensive' service and there are indications that the Conservative Government is sensitive to this with respect to the UK situation.

Table 5.1:   NHS Current Spending per Head, England (£ 1980
Survey Prices)

	Average all ages	Births	0-4 yrs	5-15 yrs	16-24 yrs	65-74 yrs	75 + yrs
Hospital and Community Health	115	645	125	50	65	225	545
Family Practitioner Services	35	40	40	25	30	40	80
TOTAL	150	685	165	75	95	265	625

Source: 'Health Care: Private and Public Spending; Resources
Needs and Provision' <u>Public Money</u> March 1982 Vol 2 No 4 p.65

One major advantage of the NHS is that it provides
a national arena in which medical issues can be
discussed. It provides a forum in which the
provision levels for the population as a whole can
be organized and assessed, in which the desirable
distribution of resources between areas and regions
can be planned, and in which responses to different
types of illness and disease across the whole
population can be looked at and debated. Such a
forum is lacking with private provision mechanisms,
where a differentiated approach and organizational
structure more naturally emerges. The NHS, as a
monopsony can also exercise its power and influence
over doctors and drug firms. It can be encouraged,
via its bulk buying practices, to put downward
pressure on the undoubted over-pricing that many of
the drug companies engage in. It has been
demonstrated that the proper organisation of this
latter aspect could save the NHS many tens of
millions of pounds a year. The drugs bill stood at
13% of total NHS expenditure in 1980 (some £450m)
second only to salaries and wages (60%). The upshot
of all of this is that the NHS is here to stay in
one form or another at least for the foreseeable
future.

5. THE TRADE UNIONS

As we shall see in Chapter 7, on the industrial front the Conservatives have continued to intervene as heavily in the economy as previous governments have done. They have changed the emphasis and form of this intervention but have not yet succeeded in cutting back overall expenditure or 'withdrawing' from intervention or regulation significantly.

The issue of the changing form of intervention is vividly demonstrated in another area where it might at first be thought a complete withdrawal was imminent. One of the planks of a 'belief in markets' is that the labour market should be left to find its own equilibrium based upon the free collective bargaining of workers and employers. Government orchestrated incomes policies should thus be avoided at all costs.

What is probably of equal, if not of greater importance here, is the political argument against incomes policies. Samuel Brittan, for instance, has argued that incomes policies practiced by Labour and Conservative governments of the Post-War period gave too much <u>political</u> power to the trade unions. His argument is that they brought trade union leaders closer to the centre of decision making where they could have a genuine and sometimes decisive impact on economic policy making (Brittan, 1981). He wants to push back such 'political' decision making in favour of straightforward 'market mechanisms', where he presumably feels trade unionists are weaker and where union leaders do not have the same political power. This kind of argument thus goes against the dominant Left position on such incomes policies: i.e. that they compromise and outmanoeuvre trade unionists in terms of political power.

As with industrial policy, however, the question this raises is whether it is possible <u>not</u> to have an incomes policy <u>of some kind</u> in an advanced industrial economy. All governments must take a close interest in what is happening to wages and incomes and the Conservative Government has been no exception to this. Take the 1982/83 situation as an instance. The public sector was working under a regime of very tight cash-limits which severely constrained wage bargaining in this sector. Employment here accounts for some 30% of total employment in the economy. In addition to this there was a highly orchestrated and government supported propaganda campaign organized to define 'acceptable' and 'sensible' wage increases in the economy generally. This was aided by the severe and something of a government encouraged recession in the economy which provided a very effective mechanism for keeping private sector wage claims at low levels. Added to this was some proposed legislation directed at the trade unions (discussed further below) designed to decrease the effectiveness of picketing and the like. All in all this added up to a very effective incomes policy despite the official rhetoric against this idea. Clearly the <u>form</u> of this incomes policy and the type of intervention that it implied was not the same as those originating during the classic period of government organized incomes policies of the 1960s and 1970s. By and large this kind of an incomes policy is an <u>imposed</u> one on the trade unions rather than a <u>negotiated</u> one with them. But it is an incomes policy nevertheless. It is also an incomes policy which avoids the political necessity of openly negotiating with the trade unions.

The issue of the trade unions is obviously an important and sensitive one in respect to the Conservatives' economic policy. They are clearly hostile to the trade unions, in line with the dominant trend in the economic advice they have chosen to listen to from academic sources as discussed above in Chapter 4. They have been at pains not to enter into industrial disputes directly.

Instead the government has 'retreated' into legislative activity to diminish the levels of legal immunities granted to trade unions by the 1906 Trades Disputes Act. The 1980 and 1982 Employment Acts made secondary picketing and secondary industrial action more difficult and also made a wider range of trade union activity subject to action under the law of torts. 'Personal and political' industrial action is no longer immune as a result, though primary industrial action against an employer is still protected from common law action (eg. strikes, blackings, work to rule, go slow). The Acts also tightened up on 'closed shop' arrangements offering immunities and compensation against dismissal, periodic votes for the continuation of closed shop arrangements and protection from activity directed against enterprises employing non-union labour. But here any 'protection' is still only afforded to those 'dismissed' in the context of closed shop disagreements. The legislation does not extend to those seeking employment, and

full closed shop arrangements are still lawful.
In some respects these amendments to the law
are quite modest in the context of the UK trade
union and industrial relations activity. They
certainly do not represent a full scale 'authori-
tarian' attack on the trade union movement. Nor
have they led to a spectacular increase in Court
activity. It is to be expected that one or two of
the more 'maverick' employers might take action
(and indeed have taken such action, eg. the 1983
'Stockport Messenger' dispute) but by and large
employers prefer to negotiate with trade unions in
the context of established and settled working
procedures. This reluctance to resort to the law
was vividly demonstrated in the case of the 1984
coal dispute. Despite considerable pressure the
Coal Board and other affected parties restrained
from using the full extent of the courts to try to
prevent secondary picketing. (Though the police
were particularly active). Perhaps ironically it
was left to disaffected workers themselves to
initiate action (at least as until September 1984).
One major problem is that the Conservative
administration insists upon conceiving of trade
unions simply as 'monopoly organizations' intent on
increasing wages, whereas they also act as central
mechanisms of representation in factory and
industry negotiations. Under almost any conceivable
political conditions in the contemporary UK,
employers would have to negotiate with their
employees over a range of issues not least the very
organization of production itself. Most would
prefer to do this with a stable and recognizable
body, which genuinely represents the workforce,
rather than on any greater individualized basis.
The 'power' of the trade unions has been more
effectively undermined by the deteriorating
condition of the economy in general, than by the
existing legislative initiatives. The argument here
is not to defend the way the Conservatives have
tried to marginalize and isolate the trade unions
but merely to point out that this is likely to be
less cataclysmic than is often recognized. In 1984
a further Trades Union Act was passed. This was
particularly concerned with the manner in which
decisions about trade union activity were handled
by the unions. It legislated for compulsory postal
ballots in the case of disputes and also initiated
a balloting procedure for the maintenance of the
unions political contributions to the Labour Party.
The Bill was passed through Parliament as the coal

dispute was in full swing, and this undoubtedly contributed to a toughening of its clauses at the time. The refusal of the NUM to hold a separate ballot on the strike, and its defeat, subsequently led to the setting up of a rival mineworkers union. But ballots are a two edged weapon. Of the twenty ballots held on the contributions issue all have so far voted to maintain the levy. However a number of employers were reported to have ended closed shop arrangements with the unions, in anticipation of the provisions of 1982 Employment Act coming into effect in November 1984.

These are undoubted set-backs for the unions, but again they do not represent a full scale and determined attempt to destroy union activity and prerogatives. The unions may be 'down' but they are not 'out'. They have suffered set-backs but the basic capacity to maintain their strength and position has not as yet been really tested or undermined.

6.   CONCLUSIONS

The Conservatives have made a number of initiatives to increase 'competition' in various areas associated with the international and domestic regulation of economic activity. These are in line with the kinds of policy advice marked out in the previous chapter. There is no doubt that these represent a significant change in the stance of Post-War governments in some of these matters but how far these will be pushed and indeed how far they can be pushed is again open to question. The consequences of these moves are also unclear and open to interpretation. On the international front as yet their stance looks cautious and modest. It has more or less supported the dominant and rather crude anti-Japanese line that developed within Europe during the latter half of the 1970s. The attempt to liberalize the international service sector is also questionable in terms of its benefits to the UK economy. It is unlikely that this will provide enough new long-term activity and invisible earnings to compensate for the disasterous fall off in manufacturing competitiveness and in associated export earnings.

On the domestic front we may see a good deal more 'privatization' and 'liberalization' in the medium term, again the full consequences of which are not at all clear. The boundary between the public and private sectors is in a period of transition and it is likely that this will be radically re-drawn during the next five years or so. But there are considerable political and economic constraints upon this process so any movement here is likely to be slow. A fuller assessment of this needs to await the further discussion of social security and taxation relationships conducted in the next chapter and also the question of industrial policy opened up in Chapter 7.

The trade unions are clearly under seige by the Conservatives, largely for the wrong reasons and with respect to what should be fairly uncontroversial measures. It is perhaps ironic that the Conservatives should be arguing so strongly for postal ballots in connection to the NUM and the unions more generally, when recent history has amply demonstrated that they have nothing necessarily to gain from this.

This chapter has also helped to consolidate a point made in other chapters. The implication of the Conservatives' moves on the economic front are not to initiate a large scale withdrawal from economic intervention but rather to change its _form_. We shall develop this point further in the context of industrial policy in a later chapter.

References

Adam Smith Institute (1984a), Trade Policy, Omega
    Report, London.
Adam Smith Institute (1984b), Health Policy, Omega
    Report, London.
Baumol, W.J. (1982), 'Constestable Markets: An
    Uprising in the Theory of Industrial Structure'
    American Economic Review, Vol 72 No.1 March
    pp.1-5.
Brittan, S. (1981), 'Why British Incomes Policies
    have Failed' in Chater, R.E.J. et al (eds)
    Incomes Policy, Oxford, Clarendon Press.
Cable, V. and Weale, M. (1983), 'Economic Cost of
    Sectoral Protection in Britain' The World
    Economy, Vol 6 No.4 December pp.421-438.
Centre for Policy Studies (1984), Making it Work:
    The Future of the European Community, London,
    June.
Dixit, A. (1984), 'International Trade Policy for
    Oligopolistic Industries' Supplement to the
    Economic Journal, Vol 44 March pp.1-15.
HMSO (1978), A Review of Monopolies and Mergers
    Policy, Cmnd 7198, HMSO, London.
HMSO (1980), Income During Initial Sickness: A New
    Strategy, Cmnd 7864, HMSO, April, London.
HMSO (1984), Building Societies: A New Framework
    Cmnd 9316, HMSO, London.
Hindley, B. (1980), 'Voluntary Export-Restraints
    and the GATT's Main Escape Clause' The World
    Economy Vol 3 No 3 November pp.313-341.
Jones, D.C. (1983), Visible Imports Subject to
    Restraint' Government Economic Service Working
    Paper No 62, Department of Trade and Industry,
    London.
Kay, J.A. and Silberston, J.A. (1984) 'The New
    Industrial Policy - Privatisation and Competi-
    tion' Midland Bank Review, April pp.8-16.
Keesing, D.B, and Wolf, M. (1981), 'Questions on
    International Trade in Textiles and Clothing'
    The World Economy, Vol 4 No 1 March pp.79.
Littlechild, S.C. (1981) 'Misleading Calculations
    of the Social Cost of Monopoly Power' The
    Economic Journal, Vol 91 June pp.348-363.
Maynard, A (1983) 'Privatizing the National Health
    Service' Lloyds Bank Review No. 148 April
    pp.28-41.
Minford, P. (1984), 'State Expenditure: A Study in
    Waste', Supplement to Economic Affairs,
    April-June 1984.
O'Higgins, M. (1981) 'Income During Initial

Sickness: An Analysis and Evaluation....'
<u>Policy and Politics</u>, Vol 9 No.2 pp.151-171.
O'Higgins, M. (1983), 'Rolling Back the Welfare
State: the rhetoric and reality of public
expenditure....' in C. Jones and J. Stevenson
(eds) <u>The Yearbook of Social Policy in Britain
1982</u> Routledge London, pp.153-178.
O'Higgins, M. (1984), 'Privatization and Social
Policy', <u>The Political Quarterly</u>, Vol 55 No.2
April-June 1984 pp.129-139.
Schott, J.J. (1983) 'Protectionist Threat to Trade
and Investment in Services' <u>The World Economy</u>
Vol 6 No.2 2 June pp.195-214.
T.U.C. (1984) <u>Textiles and Clothing: A European
Strategy</u> Congress House, London.

Chapter 6

TAXATION AND PERSONAL INCENTIVES

1. INTRODUCTION

In this chapter we extend the discussion of the
perceived role of reductions in taxation and
increases in personal incentives for the Conservatives'
economic strategy. As mentioned in Chapter 4, this
has comprised an important element in the
Government's overall 'supply-side' approach to
labour market adjustments. The government has more
or less continually argued for tax cuts and implied
that it has produced these. But is this the case?
This we look at in Section 2.

An important concept linking taxation levels
and work incentives is the idea of a 'replacement
ratio'. This also connects up to debates about the
appropriate levels of unemployment and other social
security benefits, and their supposed consequences
in reducing the incentives to work. Such replacement
ratios were developed in the context of micro-economic
studies of labour market adjustments and are also
discussed in Section 2.

One of the earliest analytical tools developed
as part of arguments for the beneficial macro-economic
output consequences of decreases in taxation levels
was the so called 'Laffer-Curve' first proposed by
the American economist Arthur B. Laffer in the
early to mid 1970s. Whilst this only had a brief
period of discussion in the UK context it provides
a useful framework in which the discussion of the
relationship between 'taxation and incentives' at
an aggregate level can be conducted. In Section 3
this analytical device is discussed and related to
the UK debate.

Finally we look at one particular taxation
reform that has been advocated by the Right and
Centre political positions in the UK - which it is

argued overcomes many of the problems at present
besetting the area of social security, taxation and
incentives - namely various forms of tax-credit or
negative income-tax schemes. The concluding section
of the chapter looks at questions of likely tax
reform more generally.

2.   TAXATION AND THE HOUSEHOLD SECTOR

In a written answer of 25th October 1982 to a
question from Mr Michael Meacher, a Labour Party
spokesman on taxation and social security matters,
the Chief Secretary to the Treasury, Mr Leon
Brittan, provided updated information on the
average tax burden for households of different
compositions and in respect to different income
levels (Hansard 25 October 1982 p.256-258). The
figures presented there differentiated between
single persons, married couples and families with
two children - these three categories making up the
classic divisions around which taxation and other
matters are generally discussed. For those then
receiving 75% of the national average earnings and
married with two children, taxation formed a 17%
real increase on the levels current at the time the
Conservatives came into office in 1978/79. For
those in similar family circumstances at the
average national wage, the increase was some 14.5%,
for those on double the average national wage it
was up by 9.5%. For those on five times the average
wage it was down by 6.5%. The figures were similar
for married couples without children and for single
wage earners. The figures for those on 75% and 100%
of average earnings included indirect taxes but
deducted child benefit. For those on 200% and 500%
of national average earnings, however, indirect
taxes were not included as insufficient information
was available on their spending patterns. Thus up
to the end of 1982 at least average taxation
burdens had increased for most sections of the
household sector except those on very much higher
than average wage and salary levels. The tax burden
on the rich had decreased.
     Despite these sharp increases in taxation
levels, however, real post-tax earnings for those
in work remained stable or rose slightly, largely
because of wage settlements in excess of inflation
rates. Thus despite the worst recession since the
1930s the real incomes of those in work have risen,
even for those on 75% and 100% of national

earnings (approximately by 1-1.5% 1978/79-1982/83).

The distributional consequences of these trends were confirmed in a comparative analysis of UK income distribution between 1978/79 and 1981/82 reported in _Economic Trends_ July 1984. Table 6.1 shows the income growth over the period for a number of different pre and post tax income levels. Average incomes showed higher growth rates in the upper half of the distribution than in the lower half. It is in this lower half that the effects of unemployment on incomes can be seen. Generally the results of the estimates presented in the article confirmed that the rich became richer - virtually for the first time since the end of the Second World War - and the poor became relatively poorer, during this period of Tory rule. The distribution of income overall became more unequal as the 'Gini coefficient' (a measure of inequality) increased by 2.5 percentage points.

Table 6.1: Income Growth at Different Levels of Income 1978/79 to 1981/82 (% increase in average income)

Quantile Group	Before Tax	After Tax
Top 1 per cent	66.4	75.2
Next 9 per cent	57.7	57.6
Next 40 per cent	43.8	43.4
Lower 50 per cent	40.2	41.1
All tax units	47.2	46.8

Source: _Economic Trends_ No.369 July 1984, Table 3 p.98.

The Gini coefficient for wealth distribution also increased between 1980 and 1982 by 5 percentage points. According to Inland Revenue statistics the share of marketable wealth (other than pension rights) owned by the poorest 75% of the population fell from 24% to 19% between 1980 and 1982. In the thirteen years from 1966 to 1979 the proportion had risen from 13% to 24%. Wealth has recently become more unevenly distributed.

Table 6.2 gives a slightly different way of

presenting the average effects of taxation changes on the household sector. It shows the changing real value of allowances against tax and the marginal tax rate for a single earner couple between 1978/79 and 1984/85. Income tax, National Insurance, VAT and other indirect taxation effects are shown separately and these then weighted to give total overall effects.

Broadly speaking the position shown here demonstrates that the marginal tax rate (the rate of tax on an _extra_ pound of income, which is thought particularly pertinent for questions of incentives to work) rose over the first three years of Conservative budgeting and has declined slightly since, though it is still not below the level of 1978/79. For the category of tax payer shown the marginal income tax rate has decreased slightly while VAT (an indirect tax) has risen over the period. These changes are only pertinent for those with an income tax liability and do not pick up on those with very low incomes or those with very high incomes. We come to this issue later. However to sum up it can be said that taxation rates and overall burdens do not seem to have decreased for the vast majority of people with the Tories but have rather _increased_ during their administrations, somewhat dramatically up to 1982 though since then there has been some relaxation in this.

This must be said with some qualification however and this raises a crucial point in discussion of taxation and social security matters. It should already be clear that a complex of differences are involved here. The tax system and the social security system are extremely complicated making it very difficult to calculate and assess accurately the full impact of any budgetary changes. There are over 45 different income maintenance benefits for instance and the exact personal or familial status of people is crucial for their liabilities to be assessed. This also helps reinforce the point that the taxation system and the social security system must be considered together in assessing the effects of either in terms of distributional and incentive issues. Here the usual threefold division referred to above as between single persons, couples and couples with children, is not a sufficiently fine gradation to capture anything like the complexities involved, let alone a single representative unit like that considered in Table 6.2 (Atkinson 1984). It is unfortunate that this complexity is often overlooked

Table 6.2: The Tax System Faced by a Single Earner Couple in the Basic Rate Band, Contracted into the State Earnings Related Pension Scheme 1978-79 to 1984-85a

	78-79		79-80		80-81		81-82		82-83		83-84		84-85	
	TCb	MRc	TC	MR	TC	MR	TC	MR	TC	MR	TC	MR	TC	MR
Income Tax	1086	29.1	963	26.1	894	25.7	811	25.7	854	26.1	899	26.2	949	26.5
National Insurance	-	15.6	-	16.5	-	17.8	-	18.9	-	18.7	-	18.3	-	17.6
VAT	88	4.4	176	8.0	172	7.9	183	7.8	173	7.7	158	7.8	144	7.8
Other Indirect	-232	10.5	-191	10.2	-182	10.2	-170	10.6	-189	10.4	-200	10.6	-232	10.2
TOTAL	942	59.6	948	60.8	884	61.6	824	63.0	838	62.9	857	62.9	861	62.1

Notes: (a) All tax credits are at 1984-5 levels deflated by gross employee remuneration
(b) TC = Real tax credit (£)
(c) MR = Marginal rate (%)

Source: Dilnot (1984) p.59.

145

by those on the Left as well as on the Right of the political spectrum, as should become apparent later in this chapter.

A particular 'perceived' problem in this connection is the so called poverty trap - a situation in which poor working families face very high combined direct tax rates and benefit withdrawal rates as they increase their incomes - which is supposed to decrease their incentive to work and earn such increased income. In some cases the combined effects of these produce effective marginal tax rates of over 100% which clearly leave such families with lower post-tax and benefit income than if they had not worked to increase their incomes in the first place. Clearly the problem here is twofold. On the one hand lower income earners have progressively been brought into the tax net as thresholds above which tax starts to be paid have risen in line with prices, but failed to keep pace with incomes. This happened most markedly in the 1950s and 1960s when incomes pushed ahead of prices. As Table 6.3 shows those with incomes at the bottom end of the distribution have been increasingly drawn into the tax net.

Table 6.3 Tax Threshold as a Percentage of Average Male Earnings

Years	Single Persons	Married Couples Without Children	Married Couples With 2 Children under 11
1949–50	39	63	123
1959–60	27	46	104
1969–70	25	37	68
1982–83	22	34	60

Note: A lower figure implies a greater number of taxable units.

Source: HMSO (1983) Table 1 p.xi.

Taxation and Personal Incentives

Focussing more narrowly on the income tax system and National Insurance contributions together, Table 6.4 shows the distribution of implied marginal and average tax rates as of 1982-83.

Table 6.4: Overall Marginal and Average Tax Rates for Married Couples with One Earner(Income and National Insurance Contributions): 1982-83

Annual Earnings (£)	Marginal Tax Rate %	Average Tax Rate %
< 1534	Nil	Nil
1534 - 2445	18.7	18.7
2446 - 11440	45.4	37.7
11441 - 15245	30.0	36.1
15246 - 17545	40.0	36.6
17546 - 21545	45.0	38.0
21546 - 27745	50.0	40.6
27746 - 33945	55.0	43.1
> 33946		

Source: Hemmings, R. (1984) Table 4.2 p.70

Commenting on this Table Hemmings suggests:

> The picture that emerges is rather surprising. Among taxpayers the lowest marginal tax rate is faced by those earning between £11,545 and £15,245 a year, and only when earnings reach £21,545 does the marginal tax rate exceed that faced by the bulk of taxpayers who earn below £11,440. Marginal rates do eventually reach 60%, but higher taxes affect only a very few taxpayers (1984 p.71).

Alongside these developments has been a growth in the provision of benefits for poor households where the head is still in full time work. These include rent and rate rebates, family and child allowances, Family Income Supplement (FIS), etc. In addition for those not in work a complex unemployment and supplementary benefits system has been developed.

One of the outcomes of the interaction between these taxation and benefit systems has been the 'poverty trap' mentioned above. Whilst often only theoretical a situation can now arise where the overall marginal tax rate exceeds 100%, whereas the top rate of income tax payable on highest earnings is at present only 60%. Table 6.5 demonstrates how

147

Table 6.5:   A 100% - Plus Marginal Tax Rate At Low Income
Levels

	Tax or Withdrawal Rate %
PAYE income tax	30
National Insurance Contributions	8.75
FIS *	50
Rent and Rate Rebates *	16.50 or 11.5
TOTAL	105.25 or 100.25

Note: * = Withdrawal of benefit rate

Source: HMSO (1983) p.xx.

this might arise.

But how serious a problem are these greater
than 100% tax rates? The Treasury and Civil Service
Commission put the number of families in Great
Britain facing this situation at between 30,000 and
50,000, not a significant figure. However, much
greater numbers of low income families could face
higher marginal rates than the high income earners
themselves. At the 50% marginal rate there are
700,000 low income families involved and only
270,000 high income ones, and at the 60% rate
500,000 low earners but only 70,000 high income
ones involved (HMSO 1983 p.xxii). It is poor
families with children that are the ones most
likely to fall into these high marginal tax
brackets since the receipt of FIS is one of the
most important conditions associated with the
poverty trap. Its withdrawal as income increases
heavily affects net income and the effective
marginal rate, as Table 6.5 demonstrates.

The question of the 'poverty trap' affects
earner families. For those out of work a different
though related issue exists. This concerns the
incentives there might be to return to work given
the existence of unemployment and other supplementary
benefits. It is suggested that just as there exists
a 'poverty trap' for those in employment there
exists an 'unemployment trap' for those out of
work. People might be as worse off financially in

work as out of work. The relationship between income in work and out of it is termed the 'replacement ratio' or rate. The higher the replacement ratio the less is the difference between net income in work to that obtained via the benefit system while out of work. The calculation of these replacement ratios is the subject of intense debate and dispute. There are a number of issues that arise here.

Firstly, replacement ratios will vary considerably between different individuals and family circumstances. The only real way to get a good idea of how important they are is to base calculations on a large and representative sample of the population at large. Grounding the ratios in actual demonstrated conditions and behaviour is to be recommended as against the construction of some system of hypothetical ratios on the basis of a presumed 'ultra-rational behaviour' by individuals.

Secondly, and connected to this, the rates are subject to great variation depending upon the causes, the frequency and the duration of unemployment (this affects the benefit entitlement profile), and depends on the actual take up of benefits to which people might be entitled. Rarely is actual take up greater than 70% of the theoretical maximum and overall the record on take up is not good (Dilnot, et al 1984, Table 2.2 p.49), though this may be better for the purely unemployment part of overall benefits.

In the third place disputes arise in connection with calculations of the relevant 'income in work.' This should include something deducted for relevant travel to work and other related expenses. But exactly how much is relevant here?

There are three main 'protagonists' in this debate. The Institute for Fiscal Studies has carried out an extensive and detailed series of calculations based upon actual samples of behaviour drawn from the Family Expenditure Survey.[1] These are paralleled to a large extent by work at the Centre for Labour Economics at the LSE.[2] Against the tenor of this work is pitched that carried out by Minford and collaborators at Liverpool University.[3] This last group works very much in terms of assuming rational behaviour on the part of agents in the labour market, which connects up to the rational expectations hypothesis discussed in Chapter 3 and to the proposals made by Minford with respect to the social security system as discussed in Chapter 5.

Table 6.6 reproduces recent IFS calculations of replacement rates as between 1968 and 1984. The results show the 'average' effect of a short period (13 weeks) unemployment and the 'marginal' effect of the 53rd week of unemployment - which is taken as an indication of the long-term position. The average replacement rates are shown for the years covered along with the percentage of the population with either replacement rates greater than 90% or less than 50% of their prospective earnings for those years. Clearly in terms of this analysis replacement ratios have been in decline since the late 1960s (though this is the period in which unemployment has dramatically increased'). Since the Conservatives gained office the short-term rates have fallen rather dramatically as earnings-related supplements to benefits were abolished in January 1982 and unemployment benefit made taxable in July of that year. Dilnot, Kay and Morris (1984) sum up on this data as follows:

> The incentive problem which existed during the 1970s - that short periods of unemployment often carried little financial penalty - has largely been removed by recent policy changes. There has never been a serious problem over longer spells: throughout the period, long-term replacement rates have been, on average, as low as 50%, and the proportion with long-term marginal rates in excess of 90% has never been above 3%. (p.59).

Broadly speaking these kinds of results have been supported by analyses carried out at the LSE's Centre for Labour Economics. But it is the Liverpool University economists who have challenged these rates. Minford et al have concluded that benefits have a massive effect upon unemployment. The estimates provided here suggest a long term elasticity of unemployment with respect to benefit levels of 2.5 (i.e. that a 1% reduction in benefit levels would produce a 2.5% increase in employment) given both supply and demand considerations. With respect to the supply of labour side only a massive elasticity of 4.5 is produced. As far as replacement ratios specifically are concerned the Liverpool modellers suggest much greater numbers with very high rates - in November 1982 they suggest as many as 22% of families had replacement rates of 90% or over (compared to only 2.2% of

Table 6.6: The Development of Replacement Rates Over Time

Year	13 Weeks Average			53rd Week Marginal		
	Average	% With >0.9	% With <0.5	Average	% With >0.9	% With <0.5
1968	0.870	35.2	0.5	0.537	2.8	30.7
1975	0.751	17.2	5.9	0.498	2.5	50.5
1978	0.790	21.0	2.3	0.519	2.2	44.0
1980	0.727	12.0	8.0	0.503	1.9	47.8
1982	0.597	3.2	28.0	0.510	2.2	52.3
1983	0.600	2.9	21.0	0.504	1.9	53.2
1984-5 *	0.590	3.1	30.2	n.a	n.a	n.a

Note: n.a = not available

Sources: Dilnot (et al) (1984) Table 2.7 p.59 and for *
Dilnot (1984) Table 4 p.61.

families in comparable IFS studies - see Table 6.6 above).[4] In addition they calculate an increase in long-term rates from 94.8 in 1978 to 106.4 in 1982 for single earner, two children households (Davies et al 1983 Tables 1 and 3). Minford et al are not reticent about drawing appropriate conclusions, as they see it, from their results. They claim that the level of benefit is a significant causal factor in the current high levels of unemployment. Accordingly a 10% reduction in benefits would reduce the total numbers unemployed by up to 500,000 over a period of two years and by more in the long run.

How then are we to assess these competing claims? On the question of the actual levels and changes in replacement ratios the important Select Committee on the Treasury and Civil Service Report (HMSO 1983) took a rather pragmatic view, but concluded that short term rates had fallen since 1979. On the longer term rates the Minford et al estimates suffer from being couched in terms of the assumption of extreme labour market rationality and high levels of travel to work expenses are assumed. But as the SCTCS reasonably remarked, echoing the Low Pay Units submission:

.....the very complexity of the system makes rational decisions about labour supply

151

virtually impossible. In addition, the scope
for individuals to adjust their working hours
to take advantage of their changing financial
position as tax and benefit rates and wages
change is likely to be severely limited. (HMSO
1983 p.xxv).

This raises the second point. The question of the
actual levels of these rates is a distinct one from
the effect they may have on incentives to work.
These two issues are often run together in the
literature. Whilst the Liverpool analysis assumes
an extreme form of 'rational action' that provides
a close causal link between these two issues, the
IFS and even the LSE's Centre for Labour Economics
also couch their analyses in rationalistic terms.
In the latter's case it is just that the rates are
calculated to be a lot lower and declining so that
the (assumed) disincentive effect is not such a
problem. In fact, as is recognised, hard evidence
on the effect of replacement ratios as such on
unemployment is very inconclusive. For instance
study after study has found no consistent results
which support a well established relationship
between either taxation increases and reductions in
work effort, or between benefit levels and the
duration of unemployment (eg. Atkinson et al 1984).
In fact in many cases the reverse is found to be as
equally likely, i.e. the probability of increased
taxes leading to greater work effort (eg. Fiegehen
1981 p.101 with respect to managerial personnel).
It is those organizations that challenge the
dominant idea of 'rationality' (like the Low Pay
Unit), that offer a radical critique of traditional
economists' views as embodied in the positions
discussed above.
Bearing this in mind, however, most observers
would probably echo the words of the Select
Committee in their summing up:

....the concurrence of a general fall in
replacement ratios since 1978 (.....) and the
near tripling of the level of unemployment
does not support the idea that high replacement
ratios are a major cause of unemployment. It
is a fact that hundreds of thousands move from
unemployment into low paid work and hundreds
more stay in low paid jobs. Factors other than
the financial one must persuade many that
work is preferable to unemployment. Among
these might be self-esteem, a sense of duty

to the community, the pressure of public opinion and the fear of prolonged idleness with its demoralizing effects. (HMSO 1983 p.xxvi).

It should not be forgotten, however, that in cutting the short-term replacement ratios the Conservatives have been following what looks like a rather classical supply-side strategy. They have eliminated earnings related supplements and introduced the taxation of benefits. These have served to, in their terms, 'increase incentives' of those at the bottom end of the income spectrum. They also cut income tax rates at the higher end of the earnings scale in their 1979 budget but interestingly enough the effects of this on incentives have not been seriously analysed at all. The concern has been almost exclusively with the lower income earners, and those claiming social security and unemployment benefits. For people like Minford et al and others (the Institute for Economic Affairs, Howell 1983) these changes are not enough, and a more radical attack should be made on the long-term replacement ratios. In this case the real levels of Supplementary Benefits - the main income support of the long-term unemployed - would look vulnerable to attack.

But why should it simply be low income families that constitute the 'problem' as far as taxation, income supplements and social security is concerned? There are a number of levels at which middle and high income earners could be included within the field of concerns with respect to these issues.

In the first place it is clear that the main burden of the recession is being borne by the long-term unemployed in the UK. To a large extent it is purely arbitrary who actually falls into a position of being long-term unemployed - there being very little that particular individuals or even larger groups can do to prevent this. In this case, on equity grounds, it might be thought a sharing of this burden more equally amongst the community would be both desirable and fair (and possibly politically acceptable?). If this is the case those still in employment and those on higher incomes should contribute substantially. It might thus seem grossly socially divisive and a 'problem', that the real income of those still in employment have been increasing during the recession and that those on very high incomes have been increasing their share of this. Higher levels of taxation would go to reduce this disparity and given the inconclusive evidence on disincentive effects, adverse work effort need not result. 'Conspicuous consumption' by high income earners in a time of recession is also to be questioned (and 'problematical') and this used to argue for some penal tax rates, rather than more generous tax advantages for these groups.

Secondly we have the issue of tax reliefs. These comprise the various income tax exemptions built into the household taxation system which are illustrated in Table 6.7.

Table 6.7: Tax Reliefs 1981-82

£ million

Pension schemes (mainly employees' contributions to pension funds)	1,000
Self-employed: retirement annuity payments	310
Life assurance premiums	530
Qualifying interest on loans for purchase or improvement of owner-occupied etc property (i.e. mortgage interest relief)	2,030
Interest on various forms of National Savings	325
Income of charities and scientific research associations	200
British government securities where owner not ordinarily resident in UK	230
Schedule E work expenses allowed as a deduction	225
Social security payments	1,060
Statutory redundancy payments	110
Others	370

Note: Social Security payments subsidy largely eliminated since 1981-82.

Source: Public Expenditure 1982-83 HMSO Table 4.9.

Broadly speaking these reliefs amount to subsidies designed to encourage various kinds of activity - they use the tax system as a vehicle for distributing the subsidies. Both the two main reliefs shown here, those on mortgage interest and on pension contributions, introduce a regressive element into the tax structure. This is because the higher the income the more likely a person is to have a mortgage, or to be in employment covered by a pension scheme.

The Conservative Government's attitude towards these reliefs has been somewhat ambiguous. Since 1981-82 the relief on social security payments has been largely withdrawn as these have been included within the tax net. In the 1984 budget the tax relief on new life assurance business was abolished. On the other hand there seems little prospect of the main mortgage or pension contribution subsidies being removed. Indeed the government increased the threshold for mortgage relief in 1982 from £15,000 to £25,000 and it is estimated that this relief alone is running at over £3bn a year in 1984. Thus it looks as though these subsidies to the better off will continue - and continue not to be a 'problem'. However these exemptions are directly equivalent to public expenditure. In principle they should be treated in exactly the same way as other public expenditure, which itself has become a central object of the government's MTFS, as discussed in Chapter 2.

If we look at the tax system overall estimates by the IFS of changes in its 'progressivity' show a small decrease in this over the period 1978 to 1983 (Dilnot and Morris 1983 p.61). Against this one might argue for a sharp increase in its progressivity. At present only some 47% of household incomes are subject to taxation so a widening of the tax base might be called for. While the 'poverty trap' has been constituted into a central 'problem' there may be a case for the deliberate establishment of a kind of 'wealth-trap' at the other end of the earnings spectrum. One way of doing this and widening the tax base would be to institute a serious wealth-tax.[5] It is important to recognize, however, that such a wealth-tax would not provide a 'pot of gold' which would easily loosen the constraints on social security spending and on public expenditure more generally. The taxation of the vast majority of tax payers with incomes of between one and two times the national average is the only source which could provide any significant relief of this constraint. In 1983 there were only some 150,000 tax payers with incomes over £30,000 for instance. For the economy overall income from wealth and other non-earned sources as presently defined account for just over 10% of GDP.

In general terms the argument here is not one designed to present an adequate 'alternative' to the present tax system. In Section 4 below we shall look at one of the serious alternatives that has actually been suggested. The objective of the remarks above is simply to question the dominant framework and the manner of approach to questions of taxation, income maintenance and social security. It is to reinforce the idea that the total distribution of incomes and family circumstances is relevant, and not just those in lower income positions. Further it is to suggest that a real commitment to providing 'social security' implies a concern with the total population and their circumstances. Those who are committed this would argue, for instance, for an extension of the level of child allowances as a right to all the population not simply to low income families, though they do recognize that this measure alone would significantly relieve one of the conditions leading to poverty. We return to this kind of argument and its consequences below.

3.   THE UK 'LAFFER CURVE'?

The above analyses of disincentive effects of taxation and government transfers were set in the context of a disaggregate micro-framework. In October 1979 M. Beenstock, then at the London Business School and later to become a Professor at the City University published an article claiming to have isolated a macro-economic or aggregative measure of the disincentive effects of taxation with respect to the economy overall (Beenstock 1979). This relied upon an econometric specification of the so called 'Laffer-Curve' developed by Arthur Laffer during the late 1970s in the U.S.A. A typical Laffer Curve is shown in Figure 6.1. It relies upon the somewhat trivial point that tax rates of zero and tax rates of 100% are likely to yield no government revenue. The function relating tax yields to tax rates is thus something like that sketched in Figure 6.1. The point of maximum tax yield is shown as X on the curve. But what is important about the way this has been illustratively used in debates about the appropriate levels of taxation is that, other than at point X, there are always two tax rates that yield the same government revenue. Thus government revenue OG for instance could be generated at either tax rate OA or OB. The argument is that after point X on the schedule acute disincentive effects begin to operate such that higher tax rates reduce government revenue.

156

With these 'penal' tax rates people either make the decision that it is not worthwhile for them to work, or they 'migrate' into the black economy. Also from the point of view of companies facing high tax rates, it is not worth employing extra labour resources.[6] Thus measured output is less than would otherwise be expected <u>and</u> government revenues begin to fall. In fact exactly the same government revenues could be generated at much lower tax rates where incentive effects are at work.

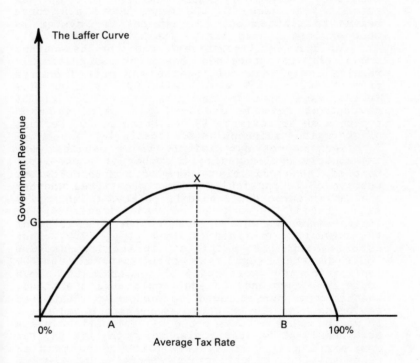

Figure 6.1:   The Laffer Curve

In popular discussion this argument has sometimes been pushed to suggest that existing average tax rates are too high - indeed that they are beyond the critical point X - so that lower tax rates would restore incentives without depleting the government's tax yield.

157

Clearly the crucial problem here is the specification of the actual curve itself and particularly its inflection point X. Whether this is a continuous curve, exactly how to specify and calculate its shape, and whether a <u>single</u> curve can adequately summarize the complex of data on tax rates and fiscal conditions are amongst the issues involved. Beenstock provided a rather simple formulation based upon time series data between 1946-77 and taking the form of a single quadratic equation specification. This produced an inflection point at an average tax rate of 60%. He goes on to point out that the present 40% (approximately)[7] average tax rate is very close to the range where his curve begins to flatten out so that the tax system is more or less at its limit. (Beenstock 1979 p.12).

As far as 'incentives' and the tax-output trade off is concerned Beenstock suggests his results imply that cutting the tax rate from its present 40% to 35% would raise GDP by about 15% (p.12), and that a marginal change in £1 of government revenue produced via raising taxes produces an approximate £3 reduction in GDP because of aggregate disincentive effects (p.13).

Perhaps not surprisingly these results were immediately challenged by a number of economists. Most of these criticisms were of a methodological character. In particular it was questioned whether the Laffer Curve could be extrapolated to encompass values beyond the range of between 31% and 42%, the limits within which the data for the generation of the curve were confined (Grinyer <u>et al</u> 1980). Thus establishing the point of inflection at 60% (outside the range) was problematical and by implication the whole shape of the estimated curve could be undermined. In addition it was questioned whether the curve could be properly identified employing time series data, as Beenstock had done, or whether such a curve could only be defined cross sectionally at one particular point in time and for one particular tax system, with a particular progressivity, distributional profile and set of labour force skills (Hemmings and Kay 1980 p.84). Thus the actual maximum point is unlikely to remain stable and a whole family of schedules would be generated as these conditions change over time. Strictly speaking Beenstock's own specification implied that the maximum would continually shift out to the right simply as time itself passed (Atkinson and Stern 1980 p.45). The results of other studies were also introduced to question the

case for a postulated maximum average tax rate of
100%, which is necessary to support the shape of
the curve identified by Beenstock. Estimates of
between 85-90% seem more plausible here (Brown,
Levin and Ulph 1976), which would alter the
conclusions of the analysis considerably. Finally
it has been pointed out that assessing the output
implication of the curve depends crucially upon
assumptions about (a) what the government does with
its revenue at present and (b) what it would do if
its revenue were cut in line with the recommendations
of the Laffer Curve type analysis. This involves
questions about comparative government sector and
private sector expenditure multipliers and about
the distributional considerations with respect to
the existing tax-expenditure regime (Hemmings and
Kay 1980, Shoup 1981).

Most of these critics supported the necessity
of more micro, disaggregated ('structural')
studies, along the lines discussed in the previous
sub-section, rather than the macro ('reduced form')
approach embodied in the Laffer Curve. Generally
they were sceptical about whether tax rates in
Britain were anywhere near levels such that the
maximum available tax revenue was close to being
reached and they questioned whether cuts in
taxation would have the beneficial effects upon
incentives or would be self-financing in the ways
suggested by Beenstock and Laffer.

A slightly more generous response to the
existence of a Laffer Curve in the U.K. context
comes from a number of articles appearing in the
journal of the Right wing Institute of Economic
Affairs. The maximum point of any Laffer Curve is
not only established by considerations of labour
supply substitution effects but also by tax evasion
and avoidance considerations. The 'disincentive
effects' of high tax rates can also lead to
unobserved or 'black economy' effects involving a
substitution of effort from the taxed to the
untaxed sector. This is something that has
particularly vexed Right wing critics of high tax
rates and is investigated by Feige and McGee
(1982). The peak of their estimated most plausible
Laffer Curve was 57% average tax rate, close to the
Beenstock one, but this was very sensitive to
assumptions about the progressivity of the tax
system and the strength of the substitution effect
to the unobserved economy. Given that the actual
average tax rate in the U.K. in 1979 was only 33%
according to their estimate - nowhere near the peak

rate of 57% - they use the analysis to point to the
effects of increasing tax revenues on a shift to
the unobserved economy and in consequence on
measured output. On average, every pound of extra
revenue raised by increasing tax rates to their
revenue-maximizing rate of 57% would cause a £1
shift into the unobserved sector <u>and</u> a 74p
shrinkage in total output of the economy (p.43).

Similar criticisms could be directed to this
analysis as were mentioned in connection with the
discussion of Beenstock above. Since the publication
of these two articles in the U.K., the aggregative
Laffer Curve type analysis has fallen somewhat into
disrepute. Whilst this is not unconnected to the
difficulties in properly estimating the relationships
involved it is also connected to the relative
demonstrated lack of success of strict labour
market 'supply-side' moves in the U.S.A. and to a
lesser extent in the U.K., in generating reductions
in unemployment and increases in output. The
increase in output in the U.S.A. economy in
particular is attributed more to 'de-regulation'
and to Keynesian fiscal management, than to
questions of taxation and incentives (see Chapter
2).

4.   A 'NEGATIVE' INCOME TAX?

The complexity of the Social Security system and
the tax system in the UK has led a number of
commentators from the Centre and the Right of the
political spectrum to suggest a radical reform of
these structures by integrating them into a <u>single</u>
and simplified system. This is generally discussed
under the heading of a 'negative' income tax (NIT)
or 'tax-credit' schemes.[8] It is argued that these
types of scheme would tackle the problems of
'poverty', of the low paid and incentives, and of
the 'inefficiencies' of having a complex, two
prolonged system as at present - all at the same
time. In addition the question of 'cost' of social
security is heavily implicated in the discussion.
In general those on the Right of this debate see
the introduction of a negative income tax system as
a means of reducing the cost of this aspect of
welfare spending and of adding to incentives to
work effects. The very recent renewed spate of
interest in these schemes is also connected to the
long-term review of social security announced by Mr
Norman Fowler in early 1984 (as mentioned in

Chapters 2 and 5). The promoters of these schemes see this as an opportune moment to lobby the government for radical changes along these lines.

The principle of the schemes can be gained from Figure 6.2. Income level OA is assumed to be some 'subsistence level' to which all would be entitled (receive tax credits). Initially after this level tax would begin to be paid along the marginal tax schedule (0)CD. Only at 'poverty income' level, OB, would the higher marginal tax rate designated by ADE become operative. There are some variations on this scheme which designate OB at the 'subsistence level' of income to which all would be entitled without paying tax. The tax schedule is then projected back through D, so that someone with no pre-tax income would receive a 'negative income' payment of OA. Alternatively the government could make up income to OB or something between OA and OB.

While it is not the intention here to undertake an extended review of the details of the various schemes proposed a number of points are worth making concerning the principles on which they are based and certain complications that would arise in the context of their implementation.

In the first place, with the simplest schemes as demonstrated in Figure 6.2, there are significant questions of the cost of the changes and the method by which they might be financed. Granting a minimum 'negative income' or 'tax credit' to all tax payers without at the same time designing some method of discriminating between poor and better off earners could be a very costly exercise and could lead to greater expenditure on welfare than at present. Thus in one way or another the simple linear scheme shown would have to be complicated by either differentiating the rates at which tax is paid as between tax payers or by having a two-tier system in which a different range of benefits is operative as between those in work and those not working for instance. This latter alternative violates the basic principles of the scheme by organizing benefit entitlement on something other than income.

The Clark (1977) and Minford (1984) proposals push for a very simple linear and 'automatic' scheme where all existing benefits are replaced by a reverse tax and a single uncomplicated tax schedule installed. In practice, as other more realistic proposals recognized, it is just not possible to render the inevitable complexity of personal situation, family circumstances, and work

Figure 6.2: Negative Income Tax

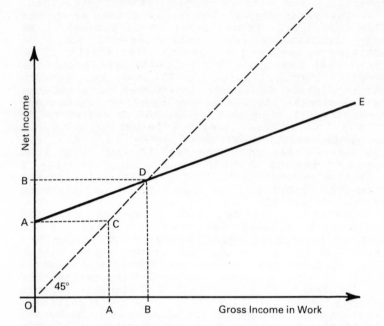

and income position into a single linear dimension. Any serious commitment to social security will require a rather complex system, even accepting that the complexities of the existing one could benefit by being realistically reduced. In the absence of this relative complexity drastic reductions in the levels of benefit would have to be instituted to produce a 'simple' system which was financially viable. This, of course, is one of the intents that accompanies the Clark and Minford proposals.

Secondly, there would be significant distributional effects produced by any change in the tax and benefit system along the lines outlined to integrate them properly. These distributional considerations are themselves complex and problematical though not very thoroughly studied. Those committed to a drastic or even modest redistribution of income and wealth in the economy have generally emphasised these complications and are sceptical about the impact of a negative income tax proposal upon this (Atkinson 1973).

162

In the third place, the negative income tax idea arose very much in the context of low income earners, the poverty trap and incentive arguments. Thus, there is relatively little emphasis on its impact on high-income earners. These once again are not a 'problem'. Considerations of the details of the schemes continually look to the lower end of the income spectrum and virtually leave out of account, other than by implication, questions of the wealthy or well off. It is only when serious consideration is given to distributional effects or ways of financing the schemes that the 'benefits' received by high income earners enter into the calculations. For instance one way of widening the tax base to finance schemes of this character would be to eliminate all or most of the present 'tax reliefs' discussed in Section 2 of this chapter and detailed in Table 6.7. This is unlikely to be something the Conservatives would support, however.

A further issue here concerns other legitimate aspects to the tax and benefit structure that debates about 'negative income taxes' tend to obscure - though this need not necessarily be the case. For instance both Clark and Minford argue that the household, as the unit of taxation, should be strengthened in connection with their proposals for a NIT. The 'family unit' is considered almost the 'natural' one from the point of view of providing some of the welfare provision at present organized via the state, as well as forming the most desirable and neutral tax unit in itself. But the tax unit is neither 'natural' nor 'neutral' in this respect. Very legitimate arguments, associated with equity and social justice, have been advanced for 'single mandatory taxation' (HMSO 1980) and any reformed system should consider these arguments seriously. Abandoning the married man's allowance - which is implied in proposals for independent personal taxation - would provide finance to increase the child allowance, for instance. It is estimated that this move alone - essentially one that could take place very much within the existing framework of the present tax and benefit system - would go a considerable way to alleviating poverty and the 'poverty trap' (if combined with the abandonment of F.I.S. - see Hemmings 1984 p.185 amongst others).

Finally we should mention a rather more implicit assumption that is built into the proposed framework of reform involving NIT. The dimension of <u>income</u> is the one thought most desirable as that around which both the tax system and the benefit system could be integrated. This coincides with the typical economist's emphasis on 'choice' and 'ability to pay' for any services received. Thus those who want to promote NIT systems also, by and large, want to strengthen this aspect of economic decision making. They see the granting of benefits in money as being the most desirable method of meeting any legitimate requirements. Recipients can then use their own discretion in purchasing the goods and services they want, as they see fit. Such proponents are therefore very much against the provision of service in kind. Indeed they generally argue that any such wider welfare provision at present organized along these lines should also be converted into a monetary or income form for recipients. But this ignores very genuine organizational and social advantage of the public provision of certain services. For instance take child care facilities as an example. It would be possible to allocate a certain part of 'negative income' or 'tax credits' for this and then let people organize their own child care facilities. On the other hand it would be equally possible not to make an explicit allowance for this as part of such a NIT scheme, but to provide such facilities directly through the Local Authorities or some other state regulated body. Which of these is to be preferred? One problem with the first option, well recognized by feminists and others, is that under such circumstances actual provision is likely to be less comprehensive than with the latter option. This is because there are all sorts of other stages and demands that enter between the granting of such income and the provision of the desired services, not least the 'politics' of the distribution of income within the family itself. Other similar cases could be cited. This, then, is an argument to restress the advantages of 'merit goods' within the welfare/social security field and for as comprehensive and universal a provision as possible. Negative income tax schemes generally ignore this aspect.

5.   CONCLUSIONS

At present the still separated tax and social security structures are in a process of being computerized - but separately. However this has given those arguing for some kind of radical tax reform an incentive to redouble their efforts since they feel that there is now at last a prospect that reforms for integration of the two systems will be more easily accepted and readily instituted. In addition the current review of these matters initiated by the Conservatives has opened a space, at least in principle, for new proposals to come forward. But it should not be forgotten, either, that proposals for large scale tax reform were put forward in the not so distant past and subsequently rather rapidly faded away. In the early 1970s a previous Conservative administration proposed a tax-credit scheme which never got much further than a White Paper. In 1978 the Meade Committee reported arguing for a radical restructuring of the direct tax system organized around an expenditure tax system amongst other things.[9] Nothing came of this, probably because of the institutional rigidities and opposition to such sweeping changes. Thus on the tax and social security front things are unlikely to change very radically or very quickly.

This is not to suggest that everything is roses in the tax and social security garden. Far from it. As Julian Le Grand has recently cogently argued, the strategy for equality as embodied in Post-War taxation and welfare legislation has more or less failed (Le Grand 1982). This alone should produce a questioning of the precepts of that strategy and open up a wider set of arguments about the long-term objectives of the system and how exactly to assess public expenditure in this field. It seems unlikely that the Conservatives will press along these lines. Their review is more likely to narrow off the options and simply reverse the existing strategy by increasing inequalities. So far their initiatives in this area have done just that, as this chapter has demonstrated. Their preoccupation with 'personal incentives', when this is precisely not the main issue, is destined to stifle any more innovative thinking and prevent it coming forward in an acceptable policy form.

Notes

1. The most up to date general survey of the IFS calculations can be found in Dilnot (et al) (1984). See also Kay and Morris and Warren (1980) and Kay and Morris (1983). Hemmings (1984) also gives a good survey of the issues involved.

2. On the LSE position see Atkinson, Gomulka, Micklewright and Rau (1984) and Rau (1984).

3. The Liverpool analysis is reported in Minford (et al) (1983).

4. Davis et al (1983) op cit and Kay and Morris (1983) op cit.

5. This is a current (1984) proposal of the Labour Party,

6. To quote Laffer himself, Macro-economic Policy in much of the Western World today consists of taxes on work, output and employment in conjunction with subsidies to non-work, leisure and unemployment. Thus it should come as no surprise that much of the Western World today has little work, output and employment and much non-work, leisure and inefficiencies. (Laffer 1979 p.45).

7. In fact this would seem to be an over-estimate of the average U.K. tax rate in the late 1970s. Others have estimated this to be between 33% and 36% (McGee and Feige 1982 p.40, Hemmings and Kay 1980 p.83).

8. The references on these schemes are numerous. For a recent elaborate exposition of the positive case for some such scheme see Dilnot et al (1984). Hemmings (1984) also gives a sympathetic summary. A more sceptical appraisal of an earlier Conservative Party proposal for a form of tax credit scheme can be found in Atkinson (1973). More overtly Right wing variants of the 'negative income tax' proposal can be found in Clark (1977) and recently in Minford (1984).

9. Meade (1978). For a criticism of this report on theoretical grounds see Prest (1979) and perhaps more importantly on grounds of organizational practicality and institutional rigidity, see Prest (1978).

References

Atkinson, A.B. (1973) The Tax Credit Scheme and Distribution of Income Institute for Fiscal Studies Publication No.9, September, London.
Atkinson, A.B. and Stern, N.H. (1980) 'Taxation and

Incentives in the U.K.' Lloyds Bank Review No.136 April p.43-46.

Atkinson, A.B. (1984) 'Taxation and Social Security' Policy and Politics Vol 12 No.2 pp.107-118.

Atkinson, A.B. (et al) (1984) 'Unemployment Benefit Duration and Incentives in Britain' Journal of Public Economics Vol 23 pp.3-26.

Beenstock, M. (1979) 'Taxation and Incentives in the U.K.' Lloyds Bank Review No 134 October pp.1-15.

Brown, C.V. Levin, E. and Ulph, D.T. (1976) 'Estimates of Labour Hours Supplied by Married Male Workers in Great Britain' Scottish Journal of Political Economy November.

Clark, C. (1977) Poverty Before Politics Hobart Paper No.73 Institute of Economic Affairs, London.

Davies, D.H. (et al) (1983) 'The IFS Position on Unemployment Benefits' Fiscal Studies Vol 4 No.1 pp.61-73.

Dilnot and Morris (1983) 'The Tax System and Distribution 1978-1983' in Kay, J., (ed) The Economy and the 1983 Budget Institute of Fiscal Studies, London.

Dilnot, A. (1984) 'The Impact of the 1984 Budget on the Household Sector' in Keen, M., (ed) The Economy and the 1984 Budget Basil Blackwell and the Institute of Fiscal Studies, Oxford.

Dilnot, A.W. (et al) (1984) The Reform of Social Security OUP and IFS, Oxford.

Fiegehen, G.C. (1981) Companies, Incentives and Senior Managers OUP, Oxford.

Grinyer, P. (et al) (1980) 'Taxation and Incentives in the UK' Lloyds Bank Review No 135 January pp.41-43.

Hemmings, R. and Kay, J. (1980) 'The Laffer Curve' Fiscal Studies Vol 1 March pp.83-90.

Hemmings, R. (1984) Poverty and Incentives OUP, Oxford.

Howell, R. (1983) 'Minority Report on the Structure of Personal Income Taxation and Income Support' in HMSO 1983.

HMSO (1980) The Taxation of Husband and Wife Cmnd 8093 December, HMSO, London.

HMSO (1983) 3rd Special Report of Treasury and Civil Service Committee Session 1982-83 The Structure of Personal Income Taxation and Income Support London HCP 386.

Kay J.A. (et al) 1980 'Tax Benefits and the Incentive to Seek Work' Fiscal Studies Vol 1

No.4 November pp.8-25.

Kay, J.A. and Morris, C.N. (1983) 'The IFS Position on Unemployment Benefits : A Reply' Fiscal Studies Vol 4 No.1 pp.74-79.

Laffer, A.B. (1979) 'An Equilibrium Rational Framework' in Kamrany, N.H. and Day, R.H. (eds) Economic Issues of the Eighties John Hopkins University Press, Baltimore.

Le Grand, J. (1982) The Strategy of Equality George Allen and Unwin, London.

McGee, R.T. and Feige, E.L. (1982) 'The Unobserved Economy and the UK Laffer Curve' Economic Affairs Vol 3 No.2 October pp.36-43.

Meade, J. (1978) The Structure and Reform of Direct Taxation George Allen and Unwin, London.

Minford, P. (et al) (1983) Unemployment - Cause and Cure Martin Robertson, Oxford.

Minford, P. (1984) 'State Expenditure : A Study in Waste' Supplement to Economic Affairs Vol 4 No.3 April-June pp.i-xix.

Prest, A.R. (1978) 'The Meade Committee Report' British Tax Review No.3 pp.176-193.

Prest, A.R. (1979) 'The Structure and Reform of Direct Taxation' The Economic Journal Vol 89 June pp.243-260.

Rau, N. (1984) 'Does Unemployment Benefit Affect Unemployment?' The Economic Review Vol 2 No.4 March pp.26-30.

Shoup, C. (1981) 'Economic Limits to Taxation'. Atlantic Economic Review March pp.9-23.

Chapter 7

INDUSTRIAL POLICY AND DE-NATIONALIZATION

1. INTRODUCTION

It would be difficult for any government in an advanced industrialized economy <u>not</u> to have some kind of 'industrial policy'. Here then is the important point, the <u>form</u> of industrial policy is what is at stake. The Conservatives have been no exception in formulating an industrial policy, though they might deny this for doctrinal reasons. It displays four main features: (a) an emphasis on new technology, particularly information processing and telematics; (b) the stimulation and encouragement of foreign firms to set up in Britain to add a competitive edge to existing indigenous firms; (c) highly interventionist manpower policies; and finally (d) a commitment to 're-vitalizing' the industrial structure through a process of extensive 'liberalization' and de-nationalization. None of these aspects formed a strong element in the Party's 1979 election Manifesto but they emerged later, if hesitantly, as central features. The Conservatives began, under Sir Keith Joseph as Industrial Secretary, with a strong rhetoric against the government playing an active role in stimulating industrial change. But they soon found that a policy of total withdrawal was neither economically nor politically feasible. In this chapter we examine the way the Conservatives' industrial policy has developed in terms of the four main areas outlined above. In addition the proposals included in the March 1984 Budget form an important element in this evolution and these form the focus for Section 3.

2. WHAT HAS HAPPENED TO PUBLIC SUPPORT FOR
   INDUSTRY?

Table 7.1 shows the industrial support programme as
outlined in the Budget Document of February 1984.
The expenditure for 1983/84 are compared to the
actual outturn in year 1979/80 when the Conservatives
gained office. In money terms overall expenditure
rose from £3.5 billion in 1979/80 to some £4.8
billion in 1983/84. Table 7.1 converts those
outturn money totals to a common 1979/80 constant
price basis via the use of appropriate GDP
deflators. While the Conservatives actually planned
for a fall in support of 36% over the three years
1980/81 to 1982/83 in fact it rose in real terms by
some 23%. As Table 7.1 shows by 1983/84 overall
support had risen by 40% on 1979/80.

Table 7.1 obviously includes more under the
heading of 'industrial support' than simply the
expenditure on running the Department of Industry
(Trade and Industry from 1982/83). It takes a wider
view of industrial support but this is appropriate
since areas like employment, energy and some of the
environmental programmes are couched in terms of
support for 'industry' in a general sense even
though they are not directly included under the
DTI's budget. Even the Export Credit Department,
shown near the foot of the Table, could have been
included.[1]

These increases in expenditure on industrial
support should be examined in the context of the
overall increase in general public expenditure
during the period of the Conservatives being in
office which were discussed in Chapter 2. With
respect to Table 2.2 in that chapter it can be seen
that overall (real) government expenditure increased
by some 10%, 1979/80 compared to 1983/84. As just
mentioned above support for industry increased by
40% over this same period so the Conservatives have
emphasized broad industrial support to a greater
extent than other areas of public expenditure.

In Table 7.1, the final column shows planned
expenditure levels for the year 1984/85. In real
terms there is a planned reduction of expenditure
on industrial support of some 7% over the previous
year levels. Such has been the typical and
consistent pattern of planned reductions over the
life of the Conservative administrations. In each
year successive White Papers have planned reductions
while in each and every year actual real increases
have emerged. (See Table 4, Appendix 1, p.23 of

Industrial Policy and De-nationalization

Table 7.1:   Public Expenditure on Industrial Support £m at
Constant 1979/80 Prices

	1979/80	1983/84	% Δ on 79/80	Planned 1984/85
Department of Trade	191	373	95	325
Department of Industry including regional and general support	1055	912	-14	710
Regional development grant	312	296	- 5	265
Regional selective assistance	54	42	-22	45
Selective Financial assist.	53	86	62	80
British Technology Group(NEB)	70	9	-87	0
Future industrial support	1	5	500	5
Scientific and technical support				
General	86	165	92	185
Space and Aero	56	66	18	68
Main 'rescue' cases	369	243	-34	62
Department of Employment	1236	2060	67	2161
Manpower Services Commission	611	932	53	996
Other (including redundancy)	625	1128	80	1165
Department of Energy	445	842	89	554
Other Departments	543	688	27	775
Scottish Office	116	126	9	124
Welsh Office	66	58	-12	58
Northern Ireland Office	308	266	-14	287
Environment (urban programme, urban devt. corporations, Devt. Commission)	99	167	69	247
Miscellaneous	-46	71	254	62
TOTAL INDUSTRIAL SUPPORT PROGRAMME	3470	4875	40	4525
Export Credit Department	-50	141	382	110
Support for Nationalized Industries*	1111	1347	21	1283

Notes: (a) *All except transport included in total industrial
                support.
         (b) Developed from Grant and Wilks (1983) Table 3 and
             The Governments Expenditure Plans 1984/85 to 1986/
             87. Cmnd 9143 Part II February 1984.

171

HCP284 1983/84 for a detailed analysis of this). Thus we should not place too great an emphasis on the likely outcome of the figures given in the final column of Table 7.1.

We can now turn to a more detailed breakdown of the figures contained in the table. It is clear that the major reduction in real expenditure has taken place within the Industry section of the DTI. But here some important internal re-organizations have been undertaken to increase support for small firms, to make greater financial assistance available to foreign owned companies in line with the second aspect to the industrial policy outlined in the introductory section, and provision for scientific and technological support has also increased relatively. In addition there has been a shift of emphasis away from expenditure at the DTI for the support of investment and into manpower support organized under the umbrella of the Department of Employment. The increase in concern with urban decay is also reflected in a significant increase in the Department of the Environment's industrial support programmes.

Despite these important changes the authors of the article on which the information presented in Table 7.1 is built and adapted stress the continuities in the range and form of support available to industry:

> .....anyone who has examined industrial support over the past decade will find that the headings, and even the magnitudes, of spending make familiar reading. The Conservatives have not, despite their earlier promises, redesigned systems of industrial support and the regional, selective and 'rescue' budgets are reassuringly reproduced, although the future of regional policy is the subject of a major policy review. (Grant and Wilks 1983, p.64).

In fact this promised regional policy review produced a White Paper in December 1983 outlining the government's attitudes and further intentions. Regional policy has been one of the mainstays of Britain's particular approach to industrial policy more generally in the Post-War period. It has absorbed a high proportion of available support within the DTI as demonstrated in Table 7.1 (between 1/3 and 1/2 of total expenditure). Table 7.2 shows the real pattern of development in this over the last seven years and it represents some important developments and departures.

Table 7.2: Regional Assistance 1977-78 to 1983-84 (All at 1977-78 outturn prices)

	77-78	78-79	79-80	80-81	81-82	82-83	(Est) 83-84
Reg. Devt. Grants	393	385	264	341	401	430	267
Reg. Selective Assistance	44	96	62	51	49	56	59
Land and Factories	52	78	88	98	105	85	63
TOTAL	489	559	414	490	555	571	389

Note: % changes: 77-78 to 82-83 = +17%
                  77-78 to 83-84 = -20%
                  82-83 to 83-84 = -32%
Source: Calculated from Table 1 Regional Industrial Development White Paper Department of Trade and Industry December 1983 Cmnd 9111.

There was a growth of 17% in regional assistance between 1977-78 and 1982-83 with selective assistance growing particularly rapidly. Between 1982-83 and 1983-84 however assistance overall decreased substantially, by 32%, though selective assistance continued to increase. It is this emphasis on selective assistance that the Conservatives wish to see developed, and this represents a major initiative in their economic policy more generally. The White Paper estimated that it 'cost' around £35,000 to create one additional job in the Assisted Areas in the 1970s (at 1982 prices) and questioned whether the fairly extensive and non-selective character of the grant system in operation since 1972 produced a net national economic benefit. It recognized that wage adjustments and labour mobility cannot be relied upon to correct regional imbalances in employment opportunities (p.3) because of structural rigidities, but suggested that the main case for the continuation of assistance was now principally a social one, rather than an economic one, with the aim of reducing regional imbalances in employment opportunities.

The White Paper argued that the existing grants schemes were heavily biased towards capital-intensive projects where grants were not necessarily linked to the creation of jobs, but might simply aid replacement investment or were directed to projects which would have gone ahead even without the grant. Under the existing arrangements the balance of expenditure was weighted heavily in favour of automatic regional development grants and was strongly biased towards manufacturing activities. The government wanted to bring in a more discriminatory structure, targeted at job creation and one extended to include appropriate service activity as well. It intended to create a structure involving: (a) approved projects which create new capacity or expand existing capacity to change a product, process or service - it was particularly looking to get more innovation based projects and to encourage indigenious development within the assisted areas; (b) it would be directed at job creation involving a limit to any grant on the basis of proven job creation effects and was likely to put a cost-per-job ceiling on the calculation of the grant; and finally (c) it would extend the scope of qualifying activities so that services could be included.

If pushed through successfully this set of proposals would quite radically shake up one of the main forms of government assistance to industry. In stressing cost effectiveness it would also likely lead to a reduction in the overall grant levels and indeed this is planned for as shown in Table 7.1, except for the much favoured selective assistance programme which is to be expanded. The proposals tie in quite closely with some other developments in the Conservatives' economic thinking, notably a re-emphasis on service industries as appropriate economic activity after a long ideological flirtation with the argument that these were 'unproductive' in some sense. The spring 1984 Budget made some explicit reference to the desirable growth of service industries and jobs. In addition its main effect was to switch emphases away from fiscal and other privileges given to capital investment and towards the encouragement of jobs

3. THE 1984 BUDGET - ITS RATIONALE

Over virtually the whole of the Post-War period there have been incentives for investment...... But there is little evidence that these incentives have strengthened the economy.......Quite the contrary: evidence suggests that businesses invest substantially in assets yielding a lower rate of return than the investments made by our principal competitions..... With unemployment as high as it is today it is particularly difficult to justify a tax system which encouraged low yielding or even loss making investment at the expense of jobs.......The importance and lasting effect (of the proposed tax and relief changes) will be to encourage the search for investment projects with a genuinely worthwhile return and to discourage uneconomic investment. (Nigel Lawson <u>Budget Speech</u>, Hansard, March 13th 1984).

The particular Budget features referred to here concern the progressive reduction in capital allowances (over two years), the abolition of Stock Relief and of the National Insurance Surcharge (a 'poll tax' on jobs) as from 1st October 1984. These measures made labour relatively <u>cheaper</u> than capital. In addition Corporation Tax Rates were to be reduced (from 52% in 1982 to 35% in 1986), though any positive effect on investment because of this was outweighted by the reduction in other capital relief measures (see below).

The conventional wisdom amongst orthodox economists is that it is high investment that provides the motor for economic growth. However, this has been subject to much qualification. In particular the role of the <u>quality</u> of investment and its attendant productivity has always been important. It has usually been assumed that during periods of rapid technological change and structural re-organization, new industries emerge which will absorb labour made redundant in displaced sectors. Thus high investment plus high productivity will produce a growing economy <u>and</u> will also produce high job creation. It seems that the depression of the mid 1970s and 1980s has thrown many of these expected tendencies into confusion and even

175

reverse. In particular, at the aggregate level, growing unemployment in OECD countries has generally meant an <u>increase</u> in productivity as a smaller labour force is deployed in relationship to a less than proportionate reduction in output. The least efficient labour and capital is eliminated, it would seem, so that the productivity of those resources still employed increases. This at the same time as economic growth rates have remained severely depressed.

These points are illustrated in Figure 7.1 for a number of OECD countries. Unemployment has increased since the mid-1970s while output per man hour has also increased. In addition investment levels as a percentage of GDP are shown for a number of countries along with growth rates for these. On the productivity/employment front it is interesting to note that only the USA shows a better position on both counts over the period. We return to this in a moment. Japan and the UK are somewhat exceptional to the general trends shown here in that Japan seems to have got the 'best' of both worlds, i.e. high productivity growth and low unemployment levels, while the UK has got rather the 'worst' of these, i.e. relatively low productivity growth and relatively high unemployment. On the investment/growth front, however, the UK is somewhat differently placed. Whilst it has the lowest growth rate of the economies specified, its investment levels are not that different to the other countries' levels. Indeed these investment levels are rather similar as between all the countries shown and do not, at casual glance at least, seem to be correlated closely to any of the other variables - particularly productivity or growth. It is this 'lack' of any clear relationship between the variables that has led the UK Treasury to question the nature and quality of investment in the UK, and to embark upon the somewhat unorthodox course of 'under-emphasizing' investment incentives.

What has puzzled economists is the seeming lack of a clear relationship between investment and growth or productivity in the UK. The UK is not that different from other economies in terms of various measures of capital stock per unit of output or per worker. (Comparitive figures are shown in Figure 7.2). Indeed it is perhaps somewhat better placed in terms of capital stock, at least for the year shown. The implication of the high capital per unit of output figures is clearly a relatively weak position for the UK economy. This

Figure 7.1: Employment, Productivity and Investment Since the Mid 1970's in OECD Countries

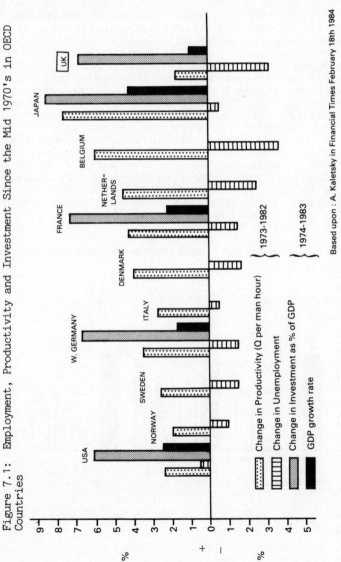

Change in Productivity (Q per man hour)

Change in Unemployment

Change in Investment as % of GDP

GDP growth rate

1973-1982

1974-1983

Based upon : A. Kaletsky in Financial Times February 18th 1984

implies a lower output per unit of <u>capital</u> figure than for the other economies shown.

Of course, this 'problem' for the British economy is not something new or unrecognized prior to the Conservatives taking office. It has been a continuing feature and 'puzzle' for almost the entire Post-War period and has been pointed to, in one way or another, by nearly every commentator reflecting on the 'plight' of the UK economy. What is perhaps different here, and which represents a more recent development, is an official decline in the expressed concern with the overall level of investment itself. Until recently the UK economy had always been chided for not investing enough. Clearly the problem with the data presented for one year as in Figure 7.2 is that it may overexaggerate the relatively healthy position of investment because of (a) the differences in employment and output levels relative to capacity in the economies; (b) the comparative exchange rate position - the pound being relatively 'overvalued' in 1980 (though the figures here were converted on the basis of the purchasing power parity exchange rates between the relevant currencies) and (c) the 'coverage' of capital stock measures at a time of shake out and rationalization.

Table 7.2: Indexes of Capital Per Worker and Per Unit of Output (1980) UK = 100

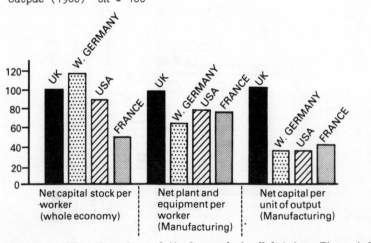

Source: 'The Heresies of Mr Lawson' A. Kaletsky, <u>Financial Times</u> April 11 1983.

Bearing these qualifications in mind, however, it has been suggested that the Chancellor sees the recent history of the US economy, as demonstrated in Figure 7.1, being something of a 'model' for possible UK developments (Kaletsky <u>Financial Times</u> Feb 18 and April 11 1984). The US economy has created some 20 million new jobs since 1973, whilst in Europe unemployment has increased. Whether by design or simply by expediency the US has become slotted into a relatively low real growth rate and low growth rate of productivity economy, but with low unemployment levels as well. Under current conditions this seems the kind of trade-off that is possible in the context of the UK as well. It is the 'labour intensive' service industries in which job growth has been concentrated in the US, and as Table 7.3 demonstrates, where additional job opportunities are thought to lie. Like the US the UK already has an extensive and relatively buoyant service sector which accounts for 61% of employment (66% in the US - compared, say, to West Germany with 49%). Given this strategy, then the issue becomes how to stimulate service sector jobs and so we return to the 1984 Budget proposals.

In the Treasury background papers to the Budget, submitted to the House of Commons and Treasury and Civil Service Committee in their investigation into the 1984 Budget strategy, a more detailed justification for the measures adopted were laid out. Table 7.4 shows the taxes and subsidies to investment, 1973 compared to 1978, for a number of industrialized economies.

The UK clearly had the highest overall tax reliefs in 1978. In addition it subsidized plant and machinery to a greater extent than other economies did in 1980. Assuming a 10% pre tax real rate of return Table 7.5 (a) shows the post tax returns to plant and machinery compared to buildings in the UK, Germany, Sweden and the USA.

There is thus a discrimination against service sectors the Treasury claims since 50% of UK manufacturing capital stock was in plant and machinery in 1980 as against 30% in the service industries. When these calculations are repeated on the basis of the relative weights of the different kinds of investment in manufacturing and commerce the figures shown in Table 7.5 (b) emerge, again demonstrating the highly discriminatory nature of subsidies to the manufacturing sector.

In addition to this evidence the Treasury pointed to the poor productivity record of

Table 7.3:   Forty Occupations With Projected Largest Job
Growth, USA 1982-95

Occupation	Change in Local Unemployment (in thousands)	Percent of Total Job Growth	Percent Change
Building custodians	779	3.0	27.5
Cashiers	774	2.9	47.4
Secretaries	719	2.8	29.5
General Clerks, office	696	2.7	29.6
Sales Clerks	685	2.7	23.5
Nurses, registered	642	2.5	48.9
Waiters and waitresses	562	2.2	33.8
Teachers, kindergarden and elementary	511	2.0	37.4
Truckdrivers	425	1.7	26.5
Nursing aides and orderlies	423	1.7	34.8
Sales representatives, technical	386	1.5	29.3
Accountants and auditors	344	1.3	40.2
Automotive mechanics	324	1.3	38.3
Supervisors of blue collar workers	319	1.2	26.6
Kitchen helpers	305	1.2	35.9
Guards and doorkeepers	300	1.2	47.3
Food preparation and service workers, fast food restaurants	297	1.2	36.7
Manager, store	292	1.1	30.1
Carpenters	247	1.0	28.6
Electrical and electronic technicians	222	.9	60.7
Licenced practical nurses	220	.9	37.1
Computer systems analysts	212	.8	85.3
Electrical engineers	209	.8	65.3
Computer programmers	205	.8	26.9
Maintenance repairers, general utility	193	.8	27.8
Helpers, trades	190	.7	31.2
Receptionists	189	.7	48.8
Electricians	173	.7	31.8
Physicians	163	.7	34.0
Clerical supervisors	162	.6	34.6
Computer operators	160	.6	75.8
Sales representatives, nontechnical	160	.6	27.4
Lawyers	159	.6	34.3

Table 7.3 (cont'd)

Occupation	Change in Local Unemployment (in thousands)	Percent of Total Job Growth	Percent Change
Stock clerks, stockroom and warehouse	156	.6	18.8
Typists	155	.5	15.7
Delivery and route workers	153	.6	19.2
Bookkeepers	152	.6	15.9
Cooks, restaurants	149	.6	42.3
Bank tellers	142	.6	30.0
Cooks short order, specifically and fast food	141	.6	32.2

Note: Includes only detailed occupations with 1982 employment of 25,000 or more. Data for 1995 are based on moderate trend projections.

Source: US Bureau of Labour, Monthly Labour Review November 1983.

Table 7.4: Taxes (+) and Subsidies (-) to Investment (as % of Asset Price)

	1973	1978
UK	-2.4	-4.4
Belgium	+0.6	+5.9
France	+1.0	+7.6
Germany	+5.9	+4.0
Italy	+12.8	+18.4
Japan	+1.4	+1.4
Netherlands	+5.0	+7.7
USA	-3.0	-0.6

Source: T & C.S.C. 4th Report The 1984 Budget HCP 341 April 1984 Appendix 10 Annex 1.

Table 7.5: Relative Tax Subsidies to Different Kinds of Physical Investment (1980)

		UK	W.Germany	Sweden	USA
(a)	Plant and Machinery	13.7	5.5	10.0	8.2
	Buildings	6.1	5.7	6.3	5.9
	Difference	+7.6	-0.2	+3.7	+2.3
(b)	Manufacturing	11.0	5.2	7.3	4.7
	Commerce	6.4	5.6	6.1	6.2
	Difference	+4.6	-0.4	1.2	-1.5

Source: To CSC 4th Report The 1984 Budget HCP 341 April 1984 Appendix 10 Annex 1 (Drawn from King and Fullerton 1984).

investment so undertaken and emphasized this at the expense of any poor investment performance overall. Comparative incremental capital output ratios, adjusted for any increases in labour use as presented in Table 7.6 highlight this feature of the UK economy. A high ICOR(L) means that output achieved per additional unit of capital has been low. This picture is only broadly indicative because it does not adjust for the different vintages of capital assets and their likely continued lives, amongst other things. However, the UK has moved from a position of a slight disadvantage to one of a very major comparative disadvantage.

The obvious question that all this poses is how successful is the strategy outlined in the Budget likely to be? To emphasise this once again, the objective is to lessen the incentive to invest in areas simply for tax relief purposes rather than for real return reasons. To do this the incentive structure is to be made more selective in the context of reducing the cost of labour relative to capital and thereby to increase the quality of investment.

One point in any assessment is that the effect may be to decrease the incentive to invest in all types of investment not just in the ones highlighted

Table 7.6: Comparative Incremental Capital Output Ratios (Adjusted for Labour Use) (ICOR(L))

| | Whole Economy | | Manufacturing | |
	1964-1973	1973-1979	1964-1973	1973-1979
UK	3.8	5.4	1.9	13.3
Germany	2.9	2.8	1.1	0.1
USA	2.5	3.6	0.8	2.0
Canada	2.3	6.5	1.2	2.5

Source: As for Table 7.5

in the above analysis. While it would seem a sensible idea to try to increase the selectivity and quality of investment, attention must also be paid to the extent of overall incentives to invest and not solely in the manufacturing sector or to those areas designated the 'innovative' ones on some fairly narrow criteria of technological advance. This is taken up below in the context of the wider stance of the Conservatives with respect to 'telematics' and other high technology sectors and industries. In general terms there would seem to be case for switching resources from 'consumption' to 'investment' in the UK economy, but it is questionable whether the measures proposed are radical enough in themselves to encourage this on anything like the required scale. It must be borne in mind that the government's main desire in this respect is to reduce their own commitments and hence withdraw from the level of support already given to investment. One effect of the measures may simply be to change the timing of investments. There is a two year adjustment period for capital allowances and Corporation Tax adjustments to take effect which might encourage a quickening of the pace of investments to gain any tax relief advantages, rather than there being any longer term real adjustments as forecast. The proposals could certainly put an end to 'leasing' as a major mode of investment finance (discussed earlier in Chapter 3). The Banks calculated that it could cost them an extra £2 billion in tax liabilities on this in 1984 as they finance most of the leasing business and will lose existing tax allowances. The exact impact on companies is

183

likely to vary depending upon the mix of tax liabilities and reliefs. As Corporation Tax is reduced and as tax liability increases with lower investment allowances companies in different sectors will be differently affected. Early estimates were that the former would not compensate for the latter so that overall post tax company profitability would decline. The Institute for Fiscal Studies estimated that companies would face a 35% increase in their tax burden overall by 1986 as more companies were drawn into a positive tax position (Devereux and Mayer 1984).

Exactly how many 'service sector jobs' are likely to be created is also open to doubt and it is interesting to note that there were no estimates of this in the Budget papers to back up the change in emphasis proposed. This represents an important silence on the part of the Treasury. The UK economy is in a different position to the US economy with respect to service sector jobs in as much that the UK economy is more highly dependent upon international trade and particularly the export of manufactured goods to maintain its standard of living. The main export item in the USA is, after all, agricultural produce. Most of the service sector's output in the UK is not internationally traded, and is unlikely to develop in this way, so that its relative growth in the UK context as compared to manufacturing output is more problematical than in the US economy, and not necessarily desirable. The service sector is also very narrowly based in terms of net international earnings. The Chancellor however believes that a declining manufacturing sector was the inevitable result of the advent of North Sea oil (Kay and Forsyth 1980). As the oil sector declines in the 1990s he sees the construction, manufacturing and service sectors picking up, but only as a result of 'market forces'. Such complacency is perhaps to be expected though not necessarily to be supported.

In a sense the strategy suggested is yet another variant of the traditional form of intervention that has typified the UK economy, as well as most other liberal democracies, in the Post-War period. It is a variant of the classic liberal 'tax-subsidy' form of intervention. It does not break with this, indeed it reinforces it, though in a different and more specialized direction. It uses fiscal incentives to try and encourage 'autonomously' organized firms to adapt their own behaviour to a more favoured position.

It neither sets up particular and novel institutional mechanisms, like the Japanese have done and continue to do, to co-ordinate individual firm's efforts or to carry some of the financing or developmental burden of 'infant' industries. Nor does it set about identifying 'gaps' in the existing productive structure and to fill them with financing and operating such productive activity itself, like the NEB was orginally designed to do, and like some 'Local Enterprise Boards' are at present doing. The point here is not to assess whether either of these are feasible or necessarily desirable alternatives, but simply to point to the basic <u>continuity in mode</u> of intervention that the Conservatives have adopted with respect to their investment strategy. In this respect the organizational structure remains largely untouched and the 'radicalness' of the approach somewhat suspect. Clearly we will have to look at other areas of industrial policy to identify more radical proposals and also provide a wider brief to assess their particular initiatives with respect to 'private sector' investment incentives. But before that, one final comment is worth stressing. If the Conservatives are to be serious about their more selective approach to investment subsidy the implication is a much higher DTI profile with respect to company scrutiny. This implies a higher level of 'intervention' into the particular characteristics of companies and their strategies and objectives, rather than less as their ideology would have it.

4. THE NEW TECHNOLOGY

In connection with the discussion of Table 7.1 above it was pointed out that expenditure on industrial support had substantially increased rather than decreased. One of the most spectacular areas in this respect has been the volume of discretionary funding for the 'glamour' industries such as micro-electronics. Whilst disaggregative studies of British industries have tended to confirm the lack of relationship between different industries capital intensities and their growth dynamic or their export competitiveness, they have tended to find substantial links between competitiveness and various indicators of 'innovation' such as research and development spending and patent licencing. This has led the Conservatives to concentrate upon such 'innovation intensive' product sectors as electronics, telematics, information systems, optic fibres and on the process innovations that connect to these, e.g. the automated office, cable broadcasting etc. In 1982 a Industry Minister was appointed with special responsibility for this area.

When the Conservatives gained office in 1979 an early victim of their Budget cuts was the Micro-electronics Industry Support Programme (Misp 1) set up by the Labour administration in 1978. Its budget was cut from £70m to £55m. But in 1984 it was announced that this scheme was to be extended and expanded in the form of Misp 2 with a budget of £120m. Along with the Micro-electronics Application Project (Map) these schemes represent the main government activity in this area, but as Table 7.7 shows by no means the only support. A quite extensive,if modest, set of programmes is under way and planned for the early 1980's.

The change of heart in these directions has a number of determinants and share a number of features. Important amongst these were the 1982 NEDO document <u>Policy for the UK Electronics Industry</u> and the 1983 report <u>A Policy for the UK Information Technology Industry</u> which called for a co-ordinated strategy in these areas, in line with what other countries were seen to be doing.[2] In mid 1982 the Alvey Committee reported (HMSO 1982a) arguing for a collaborative approach from the government, industry and the universities towards research and development in advanced information technology and programming, funded jointly by the government and industry. It suggested expenditure of some £350 million over five years to be followed by larger amounts during the subsequent developmental stages. Government financial support (two thirds) was seen to be crucial and the Committee wanted a strong central directorate to run the programme. This has been largely accepted by the government. Finally in October 1982 the Home Office published the <u>Hunt Committee Report</u> (HMSO 1982b) on the expansion of cable broadcasting in the UK.

It is around this latter Report and its recommendations that most of the public activity has taken place on the information technology and 'telematics' front in the UK ('telematics' - the integration of communications and information systems with visual displays). The Hunt Committee (which sat and reported in under six months) recommended that the UK get into cable broadcasting in a big way and as quickly as possible. The report saw this being organized largely through private sector initiatives. It suggested a locally based and single networked T.V. cable provision and operating system which would be franchised by a national regulatory body. The idea was to generate a series of commercial cable companies who would develop a system of up to 30 channels in a designated area. Each of these would be financed by a combination of rental and advertising revenue. The regulatory body would franchise each operator for a period of between 7 and 13 years, exercising only 'reactive' scrutiny. It would keep a 'watching brief' on the operations of each 'monopoly' company, exercising an 'oversight' and only react if petitioned to do so by customers or other interested parties.

Table 7.7: Principal Government Support Schemes for Innovation

Scheme	Period	Funds Available £m
Misp - 1	1978-85	55
Misp - 2	1985-90	120
Map	1978 *	85
Computer-aided Design:		
Cadmet (Manufacture and Test)	1982-85	9
Cadets (Test equipment)	1982 *	24
Cadcam (Design and Manufacture)	1981-86	16
Flexible Manufacturing	1982-86	35
Robotics	1981 *	10
Fibre Optics	1982-86	40
Joint Opto-Electronics	1982-87	15
Software Products	1982 *	15
Biotechnology	1982-85	16

Notes: * Denotes scheme runs until funds are exhausted.

Source: _Financial Times_ March 20th 1984.

187

Developments moved very rapidly in the Post-Hunt period. Early in 1983 a White Paper was issued that laid out the Government's proposals (HMSO 1983). By the autumn that year eleven licences had already been issued to companies on an initial experimental basis to develop cable networks in a number of UK towns and cities. Alongside this the Bill to set up the franchising authority was published in December 1983.

The reason for concentrating upon these developments around cable broadcasting is that they are illustrative of the style and strategy of the Conservatives with respect to economic intervention. A number of critical responses were forthcoming from amongst academics and journalists over the Hunt proposals. It was argued that these marked an end to the tradition of 'public service broadcasting' that had typified the Post-War era of visual and radio communications regulations in the UK. This commitment to a socially responsible and directive kind of regulation was to be undermined by a new aggressively commercial approach to broadcasting where regulation in the name of some 'public service' would be so minimal as to be effectively non-existent (Garnham 1983 and references therein, CSE Communications Group 1982).

In fact this kind of assessment proved false. Even the original 'raw' Hunt proposals embodied an extensive regulatory apparatus (Thompson 1983). The authors of a pamphlet published by the Institute of Economic Affairs were highly critical of Hunt on this basis (Veljanovski and Bishop 1983). They accused the Report of developing an over extensive, socially wasteful and 'inefficient' regulatory framework which itself embodied the establishment of a new series of local 'monopolies'. They argued for a more market orientated, competitive and genuinely non-regulatory approach. These sentiments were echoed by the Financial Times in commenting upon The Cable and Broadcasting Bill which was published in December 1983 (Financial Times December 2nd 1983). It argued that excessive supervisory control over the franchise holders was embodied in the Bill's clauses and that the proposed authority would be given enormous discretion when it came to the granting of licences. Altogether too much power was to be lodged in the authority. It would become just another IBA - though it would not be responsible for actually transmitting the programmes. Once again a similar form of regulatory intervention had emerged despite a rhetoric to the reverse.

The additional importance of cable broadcasting is that it represents the strategic manner in which the government hopes to generate a domestic information technological base. It is central to its conception of 'industrial policy' in this area. This is to be led by making available a wide range of new entertainment channels to domestic consumers. Viewers of popular television programmes will in this way finance the investment in a new generation of interactive, two-way communications networks which it is hoped will be attached to these systems. This is the way 'telematics' is to be consumer led in the UK.

The question here is whether this entertainment-led approach will be at all successful. It is not clear that there is a widespread demand for cable systems, given the level of already existing broadcast entertainment and information channels available to households (four national networks, two existing information channels, and increasingly a 'video channel'). Financing these through rentals and advertising looks uncertain in the context of the initial capital costs and the rapid exhaustion of new sources of advertising revenue.

A more sensible approach would have been to have developed an initial interactive cable network for commercial users only, linked to the British Telecom telephone system. This would have tapped a more stable source of revenue and would have provided the basis for a genuinely national network. It would have given a fillip to the experimental development of new cable technology without getting locked too early into any particular single one of these at a time of rapid technical change. As it stands such opportunities seem to have been missed. The UK could as a result be saddled with a very patchy network, with little consistency between its parts, and with an outdated technology arising from the commercial pressures on companies to go for tried and tested cable systems rather than the more advanced and risky ones.[3]

In fact from early 1984 there were increasing signs that the whole Cable Broadcasting initiative was drying up largely because of 'lack of demand'. Both McKinsey management consultants and CIT Research reported that profitability was unlikely to emerge from the entertainment side of the business and that the number of UK subscribers to cable TV could actually be less in 1990 than it was in 1980. The area is a high capital cost, very high risk venture, in which poor quality management expertise has been attracted. The 1984 Budget, by withdrawing investment grants, made prospective financial problems even worse. Both reports predicted heavy losses to the companies involved. American and Canadian experience in cable broadcasting is difficult to assess because of the different regulatory environments in operation or proposed. A recent study points out that profitability is highly 'regulation sensitive' in these countries but that actual profitability (apart from one or two exceptions) has been low or non-existent (Perrakis and Silva-Echenique 1983). The government in the UK tried to re-stimulate the flagging momentum of development by stitching together an uneasy alliance between the BBC and ITV companies in the spring of 1984, to run what was described as a basically unprofitable satellite broadcasting company to feed into cable networks. It was later confirmed in newspaper reports that this company was also likely to make considerable losses. All in all, then, this particular area of 'industrial policy' seems to be foundering under an overambitious and too rapid build up in the face of what looks to be an indifferent consumer demand. In addition direct satelite broadcasting looks cheaper to mount than an extensive cabling alternative.

What this emphasis on the 'consumer end' of the telematics strategy also leaves out of account is the issue of a co-ordinated or coherent approach to the 'production end'. Here the Conservatives are much more vague and uncommitted - largely relying upon their grant programme for investment as outlined above when discussing Table 7.7. The approach here seems deliberately underplayed. The Technology Minister Mr Kenneth Baker was reported to have commented We are no longer in the business of grand strategies. We work from the bottom up (Financial Times September 21 1983). But it is not clear what role the promised 'de-monopolized' British Technology Group will fulfill (the old NEB) and INMOS, the state owned chip producer exists in a very uncertain financial and organizational environment while the government decides on its ownership future. In May/June 1984 first the American company AT & T and then Thorn EMI made strong bids for INMOS but the government dithered in the face of the likely locational output consequences of both bids. Thorn subsequently won control of INMOS. Meanwhile chip 'famines' come and go. There seems no mechanism envisaged which can plan ahead for chip production. As a result the semi-conductor supply cycle has moved with extraordinary speed from boom to recession and then back again to boom, and promises to continue in this mould. In the meantime small 'venture capital' firms are the ones to be encouraged to pick-up on innovative technological developments in these fields. Any overall management strategy is neither desired nor likely to emerge.

As a consequence of much of this, while the information technology industry has shown rapid growth rates of an average 16% per year between 1973 and 1983, employment in the industry has stablized and import penetration has grown. A further NEDO study of the industry published in August 1984 pointed out that the supply industry was weak in international terms (NEDO 1984a). Much faster rates of growth typified foreign industries such that the UK share of the aggregate output of the USA, Japan, France, West Germany and the UK together had fallen from 9% in 1970 to 5% in 1983. Imports accounted for 54% of the UK market and were on a growing trend (29% in 1970) and the trade deficit stood at £800 million in 1983. The main UK companies were small by world standards and its innovations were taking longer to be developed into products. All in all Britain's prospects looked bleak.[4]

5.   OTHER INDUSTRIAL SECTORS

The Conservatives have been much taken by the prospects of 'new technology' not just in the areas concentrated on above but in advanced medical technology, in bio-technics, computer aided design and so on. These are important areas and not to be neglected. They are difficult to co-ordinate or 'plan' comprehensively precisely because uncertainties are rampant and change rapid. Until these technologies 'settle down' it is perhaps wise to take an arms length approach, though this is not to suggest that a much more active stance should not be, and indeed could not be developed with respect to 'production end' initiatives.

But what is more problematical is the over-concentration of this area almost to the exclusion of other perhaps more important areas of industrial and manufacturing activity. In the short to medium term, and longer term in some cases, there are a range of already well established

191

production activities which would require close scrutiny and attention, but these have been virtually ignored by the Conservative government. It has neglected, some would argue deliberately neglected, large sectors of basic employment maintenance or even employment generating manufacturing activity, like heavy mechanical engineering, textiles and clothing, white goods industries, food processing, chemicals, synthetic textiles, prefabrication and construction activity and so on, much of which has a strong international trading element or which might develop in such a direction. The mesmerization with a limited area of 'new technology' and a head-long rush into service sectors has virtually eliminated the bulk of British manufacturing industries from any kind of serious attention and help at a micro-level.[5] Here we concentrate on just one of these areas to highlight some of the problems it faces and the tendencies under way.

Table 7.8 sets out the European market for domestic appliances in 1978 and 1983. It shows a stagnant demand. In part this is due to the recession in consumer spending, but it is also due to the 'maturing' of the industry, resulting in a saturated market penetration as the traditional 'S' (or logistics) curve flattens out at higher per capita income levels. There are some areas of possible growth, however, e.g. the first three items in the Table, and a basic replacement demand for the others.

Table 7.8: European Market for Domestic Appliances (Millions of Unit Sales 1978 and 1983)

	Freezers	Dish Washers	Micro-wave Ovens	Refri- gerators	Washing Machines	Cookers (incl. built-in)
1978	3.8	1.89	0.2	9.6	8.5	8.0
1983	3.5	1.9	0.8	9.6	8.35	7.35

Source: C. Papaport 'European Domestic Appliance Industry' Financial Times February 20th 1984 p.14.

The conditions in the industry are ones of considerable over-capacity - 15% to 30% for most firms - and low profit margins. In addition Eastern imports are increasing rapidly at the cheaper end of the fridge and cooker market where they now have some 10% share in the UK, France and Germany. In addition to this it is the Japanese who have captured the only real growth sector - micro-ovens. They account for 70% of this market in the UK and 50% in Europe as a whole. They also intend to expand their penetration of the refrigerator and freezer market particularly in the UK and Germany.

The European supply-side was until very recently made up of seven dominant companies and some 350 smaller ones. Electrolux (Sweden), Phillips (Holland), Siemens-Bosch (Germany) and Zanussi (Italy) all held about 12% to 13% of the market each. Behind these came AGE-Telefunken (Germany), Thompson-Brandt (France) and Indesit (Italy) with about 5% each. The largest British manufacturers (Hoover and Thorn-EMI) are among the smaller companies with about 3% to 4% of the market, though they are stronger just in the UK.

Given this market structure there were two tendencies in hand. One involves cut-throat competition and the other cartelization. In fact these are tending to develop in parallel. Competition was taking the form of attempts to 'upgrade' the technology of existing products and innovations in developing new ones rather than by price cutting. The technology for most of the goods produced in this area has been in existence for some 20 years, but Zanussi and to a lesser extent Hoover pinpointed a market segment for high quality, micro-electronic enhanced machines. Innovations like new ways of washing clothes with sound vibration are still in the experimental stage. Cartelization, on the other hand, led to a series of bilateral talks between manufacturers (Zanussi, Thompson-Brandt and Phillips in particular) on agreements to reduce capacity and to divide up the existing stagnant market between themselves. In addition Japanese liaisons are high on the list of possible developments. Co-operation and vertical integration with distributors is also on the increase in an attempt to consolidate and strengthen market share. The Japanese could easily pick up a manufacturing base in Europe relatively cheaply given the 'semi-redundant' capacity available. But any cartelization was hindered until recently by the lack of a clear cut industry leader. This may emerge in the near future however since Zanussi went bankrupt in 1984 and was taken over by Electrolux. Given this there has been some talk of the EEC taking an initiative rather than letting the situation develop into a more desperate or chaotic state.

This latter point is important since it may to some extent take the issue out of the hands of the UK government altogether. The Conservatives have no discernable consistent position on these kinds of developments though they are likely to become increasingly important. The EEC has already made major initiatives on European steel rationalization (Chapter 5), though the UK government proceeded on its own programme of capacity reduction to some extent ahead of a properly devised European approach. This meant that the equivalent capacity that the French and Germans were 'putting on the table' when negotiations got fully under way had already been eliminated in the UK by prior domestic interventions. As a result the UK's bargaining position was weaker than it might otherwise have been. The general point here is that the way these developments, and others where the EEC has shown an interest and where tendencies towards cartelization or integration are arising, actually turn out could have a major impact on the UK economy with respect to job maintenance and trade possibilities. Yet there is little sign that this is receiving the recognition it deserves, if any at all in the UK. A serious industrial policy under present conditions should look at the whole gambit of manufacturing activity and at the international market developments in hand and possible tendencies in these. All this is to be left to the 'free play of market forces' when it is clear that this is both not possible and actively being undermined in the context of European 'co-operation' (see also Owen 1983).

In fact it is these kinds of genuinely 'strategic' considerations that are perhaps more important for an industrial policy than, say the concern about how many industrial robots are being installed in British Industry, or even about the detailed levels of subsidy for different kinds of 'new technological' investment. Table 7.9 shows the World distribution of 'robots' in 1981 and 1983. Robot is a difficult term to identify and national definitions vary a great deal, though Japan leads whatever source is consulted. Sweden has the highest per capita robot population. Clearly, although Britain lags somewhat behind West Germany, it is not that far out of line with developments in other countries. This quite rapid rate of build-up in the UK is confirmed by a recent large scale survey which predicts a doubling of the use of micro-electronics in industry between 1981 and 1985 (Northcott and Rogers 1984). All in all then there seems little reason to think that the UK is doing very much worse than its competitors on this score, and it is difficult to see what an extension of 'industrial policy' in this limited area could add to existing efforts. The question is more one of which strategic areas need some stimulation, why and under what conditions.

Table 7.9: World Robot Population 1981 and 1983

Country	Estimated No. of Robots Installed 1981	1983
Japan	14,000	16,500
USA	4,100	8,000
West Germany	2,300	4,800
Sweden	1,300	1,900
UK	713	1,750
France	620	1,500
Italy	450	1,800
USSR	200	na
Other Countries	1,200	na
TOTAL	24,883	na

Source: Economist Intelligence Unit Chips in Industry Special Report No.135 1982 Table 13 p.45, and N.G. Attenborough 'Employment and Technical Change: The Case of Micro-electronic Production Technologies in UK Manufacturing Industry'. DTI Government Economics Service Working Paper, No.74 1984.

6. DE-NATIONALIZATION

The comments made about British Telecom above in connection with the Conservative efforts to develop a consumer-led 'information technology' strategy in the cable broadcasting area raise another aspect of their industrial policy, namely de-nationalization. British Telecom is one of the prime targets in this respect. The nationalized industries seem to be the major monopolies in the economy and their de-nationalization will contribute to its re-vitalized and newly competitive structure. Whilst these kinds of comments about the benefits of such a policy might seem rather vague, they are about all the justification that has actually been offered. Very little detailed arguments about benefits have been provided and the de-nationalization seems to be proceeding on the basis of largely doctrinal expedients.

In Table 7.10 the results of the de-nationalization programme to date and the likely prospects up to the next general election are detailed. Looking first at the top half of the table a number of points are worth making about the activities involved.

Table 7.10: The Privatisation Programme

Sale	Amount (£m)
1979/80	
5 per cent of BP	276
25 per cent of ICL	38
Shares in Suez Finance Company and miscellaneous	57
1980/1	
50 per cent of Ferranti	54
100 per cent of Fairey	22
North Sea oil licences	195
51 per cent of British Aerospace	43
Miscellaneous and small NEB interests	91
1981/2	
24 per cent of British Sugar	44
55 per cent of Cable and Wireless	224
100 per cent of Amersham International	64
Miscellaneous plus Crown Agent and Forestry Commission land and property sales	204
1982/3	
51 per cent of Britoil (first cash call)	256
49 per cent of Associated British Ports	46
BR hotels	34
Sale of BA subsidiary, International Aeradio	60
Sale of oil licences, oil stockpiles and miscellaneous	108

Table 7.10 (cont'd)

Sale	Amount (£m)
1983/4	
Second cash call for Britoil	293
7 per cent of BP	565
25 per cent of Cable and Wireless	260
Miscellaneous (estimate)	132
1984/5	
100 per cent of Enterprise Oil	392
50 per cent of Wytch Farm	215
48.5 per cent of Associated British Ports	52
76 per cent of Inmos	95
100 per cent of Jaguar	297
100 per cent of Sealink	66
British Telecom (first cash call)	1,506
Sale of oil licences and miscellaneous (estimate)	160
Planned sales (estimates)	
1985/6	
48 per cent of British Aerospace	350
British Airways	800
British Telecom (second cash call)	1,205
British Airports Authority	400
British Shipbuilders warship yards	200
1986/7	
British Telecom (third cash call)	1,205
Royal Ordnance Factories	300
Unscheduled	
(i) Parts of the gas and electricity industries, plus smaller enterprises including National Bus, Land Rover, Rolls-Royce, Unipart, British Steel's profitable business, British Nuclear Fuels	4,000
(ii) Possible dilution of holdings in denationalized companies	1,200

Source: <u>Midland Bank Review</u>. Spring 1985 p.19.

In the first place they represent activity which was reasonably buoyant under the depressed conditions of the early 1980s (electronics, computers, oil). Secondly a number of these organizations were either originally private ones taken into public ownership during the late 1970s because of temporary financial difficulties (ICL, Ferranti) or were ones developed around North Sea Oil activity. They did not involve the traditional, immediate post Second World War nationalized industries (other than with respect to rather marginal activities such as BR hotels or the National Freight Corporation). The 'core' or 'Old Guard' nationalized industries escaped relatively unscathed during this period. Finally, whilst in a number of cases the state withdrew from a controlling interest in the companies it did not abandon its stake altogether. In fact it probably remained the largest single, and therefore dominant shareholder, even though it did not form a controlling 51% or over of the capital stock. (Additional parts of these holdings may be sold in the future).

What about the prospects for the other, more traditional nationalized industries? The situation with respect to these is set out in the bottom half of Table 7.10. To privatize these was proving something of a more complex and difficult task. It is not easy to dispose of very large sections of productive activity during a period of instablility and depression. A great deal of discussion was underway though action to push through these proposals was not lacking in the early part of 1984. As it stands it looks as if British Telecom, British Airways and The British Airports Authority could be fully privatized before the end of 1986. Of course this still leaves a very large section of the present nationalized industries virtually untouched, a number of which are mentioned in the Table under the 1986-87 and Unscheduled proposals. In particular the 1982 Transport Act enables the National Bus Company assets to be sold and it looks as if the Inter-City coach business will be the first part to go. There is in addition the prospect of a sale of some of the CEGB generating capacity and elements of the Gas industry could also be de-nationalized.

To privatize all of this activity would represent a very radical withdrawal of state ownership over large sections of British Industry, though whether this will also herald a disengagement of intervention and regulation is something of another matter. The most likely outcome of the proposed measures would be to generate a series of very large and dominant <u>private</u> monopolies rather than state-owned ones, as commentators from both the Left and the Right of the political spectrum have not failed to discern. Thus one of the ironies of the Conservatives' policy here is that in the name of 'liberalization' and competition the government could be about to create companies whose activity it will then have to closely regulate. In the case of British Telecom (BT) for instance an Office of Telecommunications was set up to supervise BT and its small competitor Mercury. Mercury is not going to develop an extensive range of facilities despite government encouragement to do so but will rather confine itself to a limited set of profitable 'trunk' and inner-city services. The government has also given assurances that other companies will not be allowed to set up in these areas for at least seven years. The dominant market position of BT will therefore be preserved. In fact there will be great incentives for collusion between Mercury and BT to 'carve up' the overall market in some satisfactory way between themselves.

Similar problems beset the privatization of other nationalized industries. British Airways (BA) will offer a formidable challenge to the UK independent airlines. As a private business it is likely to consolidate and develop its market share. This led some of the independent schedule carriers (e.g. British Caledonian) to call for the breaking up of the BA network and a parcelling out of some of its routes to them prior to sale. Without this they feared that a privatized BA would soon come to dominate the market and begin to operate as a monopolist, forcing the independents out of business. But again such a <u>duopoly</u> situation would not seem a great improvement over a monopoly one.

The proposals the government made concerning these issues in their July 1984 White Paper (CAA 1984) caused a political storm. All BA's provincial and Gatwick Airport short-haul routes were to be transferred to the independent airlines, lock, stock and barrel, plus a smaller number of long-haul routes. The idea was to strengthen the base route network of the 'independents'. However these independents themselves were in a delicate position as the smaller companies among them feared a British Caledonian 'take over' of the more profitable routes. In addition simply transferring rights to routes from one airline to another would not seem to increase 'competition' as BA was quick to point out. It offered 'double designation' on the routes involved, but this was rejected by British Caledonian. While the outcome of these arguments is still in the balance it looks as though in one way or another BA will retain most of its route network intact prior to its de-nationalization in 1986. Meanwhile all this must look rather odd to BA's international 'rivals'. The Conservative Government's obsession with breaking up BA could play directly into the hands of other European airlines who are not faced Industrial Policy and with such a politically motivated threat.

In the case of the National Bus Company its inter-city business (National Express) has consolidated its market share since the liberalization of route licencing in 1980 and is now increasing its domination of the market.

All these developments bode ill for a supposed increase in competition. It must be accepted however, that the early liberalization in some of these areas during the 1980s did produce some short-term consumer gains, e.g. on densely used internal bus and air routes - though probably at the expense of less densely used inter-urban and rural routes (Bagwell 1984). But the uncertainty surrounding the new moves has led most critics of the government to strongly suggest that the real motive for the de-nationalization programme is to raise money to offset government borrowing rather than to increase competition. Given the government obsession with the PSBR it is estimated that some £7.5 billion could be raised to offset this over the next 5-6 years. Clearly there is an incentive to protect the scale of operations of the industries if the government is to attract the maximum revenue at the time of their sale. Opening up the possibilities of greater competition will make the acquisition of their assets a less attractive propostion for private financial interests. There is the added complication that a floatation of such large amounts of share capital as will be involved, over a relatively short period of time, will add downward pressures on the price that can be obtained. This may also disrupt the possibilities of raising additional external finance for already existing companies or other new ventures. By and large the timetable of the de-nationalization programme has been devised in the light of the finance it will raise for the Government which means that a lower price will be obtained for the assets floated than with a programme timetabled flexibly to meet market demand.

In fact the government has had to extensively 'massage' the balance sheets of a number of the candidates for de-nationalization in an attempt to make them an attractive proposition to private finance. Thus British Airways saw a massive 'capital restructuring' in the late 1970s/early 1980s to progressively write down the value of its assets and thereby eliminate large amounts of debt burden (though it still has significant amounts of this). The British Airports Authority has virtually become a totally internally financed organization by switching to current cost accounting and in this way has built up large capital reserves from which investment can be undertaken. The resulting minimal 'external debt' makes it a particularly attractive proposition. Nor has the government shown great aptitude in managing the sale of its assets as the Amersham International float of 1982 demonstrated. It drastically underestimated the value of the company's assets such that the privately owned share prices immediately rose well above their offer price (from 142p to 292p per share). In 1984 the floatation of Enterprise Oil was not handled any better. When Rio Tinto Zinc - a large mining based conglomerate - applied for 49% of the shares the government stepped in to prevent such a large stake going to one bidder with the result that underwriters were left to pick up some 40% of the shares that remained under-subscribed.

All this should severely undermine the claim that these sales are proceeding purely in the name of increased competition and industrial rejuvenation. In general terms it is not clear what overall benefits will be generated by the change in ownership of the nationalized industries, or in the sale of assets to finance current government expenditure. This looks to be just another indirect 'subsidy' to consumption via tax cuts. The lack of a real competitive edge in the current round of de-nationalization has been well recognized by commentators of the Right. After a somewhat tentative and critical analysis of the present proposals Samuel Brittan could only propose a pro-rata 'give away' of shares to all citizens so as to realize the dream of (once again?) a genuinely 'property owning democracy'' (Brittan 1984).

7. OTHER DISCRETIONARY SUPPORT

As was pointed out above and in the context of Table 7.1 the volume of discretionary funding to support and promote investment in general manufacturing industry is under severe pressure, despite its central importance to the economy. The only serious response in this area has been with respect to another aspect of the government's industrial policy, namely the encouragement of foreign firms to set up plants in Britain. Expenditure in this area has increased but it is still only marginal to other areas of support. This part of the policy attracts a great deal of publicity which nevertheless far outweighs its real significance. For instance, the deal with Nissan in 1984 to set up in Teeside attracted a subsidy of some £5 m. for the creation of possibly 800 jobs, but other indigenous motor component manufacturers

Table 7.11: Private Sector Investment Abroad and Overseas Investment in the UK: 1979 - 1983 (£ millions)

	1979	1980	1981	1982	1983
Investment Abroad:					
Direct	31,570	34,130	45,530	55,550	62,910
Portfolio	12,000	18,100	24,600	38,200	57,700
TOTAL	43,570	52,230	70,130	93,750	120,610
Overseas Investment in UK:					
Direct	21,880	26,440	29,520	31,240	35,370
Portfolio	4,530	5,100	5,800	6,800	9,600
TOTAL	26,410	31,540	35,320	38,040	44,970
UK Net Investment Abroad:	17,160	20,690	34,810	55,710	75,640

Source: BEQB June 1984, Table G, p.228

attacked this, arguing that they could have created more jobs for less money. However this is to miss the main point of the government's initiatives in this area. British industry lacks a competitive edge, something which foreign firms with different styles of management, different methods of financial control and embodying 'best practice' production techniques, might be able to inject into the UK economy.

However, this all needs to be put into perspective. Table 7.11 shows the levels of private investment overseas and that attracted into the UK, over the period of the Conservatives being in office. As can be seen from the bottom line of the Table there is a massive accumulated net outflow of investment which has been steadily increasing under the Tories. In 1983 this accumulated net outflow reached over £75 billion.

8.   EMPLOYMENT SUPPORT

One other element that has grown massively during the period of the Conservative administrations - something that we might consider as a fourth arm to their 'industrial policy' - is expenditure on manpower services. This escalated from £125m in 1974 to £1.4 <u>billion</u> in 1982/83 and threatened to increase to £2 <u>billion</u> in 1984/85. The main area of the labour market to which this expenditure has been directed is at youth training. The numbers of young people entering into the various schemes grew from 216,000 in 1978/80 to over 550,000 in 1981/82. Britain now has one of the largest short-term youth and manpower schemes in Europe.
      The context to the rise of these measures can be seen from Table 7.12. Youth unemployment has grown rapidly in OECD countries over the period of the depression, faster than unemployment in general, and is now relatively more significant than general unemployment levels. The UK displays one of the worst records. The various 'youth training' schemes have been a short-term amelioratory response to this trend in the UK case.

Table 7.12: Youth Unemployment in Selected OECD
countries (%)

Country	1979	1980	Year 1981	1982	1983	1984
USA	11.3	13.3	14.3	17.0	16.4	13.3
Japan	3.4	3.6	4.0	4.4	4.5	4.9
Germany	3.4	3.9	6.5	9.5	10.8	10.1
France	13.3	15.0	17.0	20.3	21.1	26.1
UK	11.6	15.3	19.8	21.6	22.7	21.8
Canada	13.0	13.2	13.3	18.7	19.9	17.9
Italy	25.6	25.2	27.4	29.7	32.3	34.1
Total of %s	10.9	12.4	14.0	16.5	16.7	15.5

Source: OECD Employment Outlook September 1985. Table 7 p.19

The special employment measures more generally that
were in operation as of 1982-83 and their gross
expenditures were as follows:

1. Temporary short-term working compensation
    scheme (£113m): This encouraged work
    sharing through short-time working thereby
    averting impending redundancies.
2. Job release schemes (£244m): This reduced
    the supply of labour by encouraging early
    retirement.
3. Young workers (£59m): Stimulated the
    creation of jobs for young people by
    increasing their competitiveness in the
    labour market.
4. Community programme (£175m): Provided
    labour for community orientated projects.
5. Youth opportunity schemes (£692m): Provided
    unemployed young people with a period of
    work experience and practical training.

In October 1982 there were some 645,000 people on
these SEM schemes.
    As a result of the White Paper A New Training
Initiative: A Programme for Action (Cmnd 8455
December 1981), the YOPs and Unified Vocational
Preparation Programme (UVP) were abolished in

September 1983 and replaced by the Youth Training Scheme (YTS). This provides a guaranteed twelve months training to all sixteen to eighteen year old unemployed people. They are paid an 'allowance' of twenty five pounds per week while the government provides an additional grant to employers of £1,850 per place per year. New entrants to this scheme were expected to be around 460,000 in the first year.

This represents a massive and rapid build up in support and in intervention in the labour market. Against criticism from the Right the Treasury has justified this in terms of its supposed distributional benefits. It trades a curtailment of the market adjustment process in return for a more acceptable distribution of unemployment. Whilst critics of these schemes from the Left have seen them as simply a way of reducing the price of labour associated with certain types of employment and in certain sectors of the economy, this is not altogether true. Such schemes as the Young Workers Scheme have been designed for this purpose though some of the others lessen the impact of unemployment on earnings by keeping earnings up. Other schemes delay redundancy rather than avoid it (e.g. TSTWCS)

The general question this poses, however, is whether these large sums have been well spent. It would seem rather pointless to fund the training of personnel if they cannot then go on to find employment when they leave. Increasingly this has become the case in the UK, as a glance at Table 7.13 demonstrates. As unemployment has risen (while vacancies remained static or decreased) the percentage of YOPs entrants in this case, who have been able to find jobs has fallen to below 50%. This demonstrates a peculiarly one sided approach to unemployment relief - a massive training scheme but little and indeed decreasing funding to generate jobs. The UK also lacks a long-term vocational education and training scheme (NEDO 1984b), though it might be possible to transform the essentially non-directional and foundation experience YTS into such a scheme to orientate it more towards occupational competences.

One positive feature of the Conservatives' approach, however, has been the way they have disengaged their forward looking industrial policy from a concern with simply maintaining employment. Their investment orientated moves and rationalization initiatives have been undertaken independently of

Table 7.13:   Post-YOP Placement Record

Of the Number Entering YOP Schemes on:		% in work or education On Leaving 6 Months Later		% unemployed (Nationally)
Sept./Oct	1978	75	78	5.1
January	1979	64	66	5.4
March/April	1979	62	67	5.8
June/July	1979	61	64	6.3
Sept./Oct	1979	65	68	7.4
January	1980	51	51	8.4
March/April	1980	49	50	9.5
April/June	1980	42	45	10.2

Source: Rodney Stores 'Spending on Youth Employment: Is it Worth it?' Public Money, Vol 2 No 1 June 1982, p.33.

the requirement to preserve jobs. In a sense then they have disengaged their 'employment policy' for their 'industrial policy' - a problem that has beset Post-War industrial policy more generally.

9.   CONCLUSIONS

The Conservatives have developed a highly active and interventionist 'industrial policy' since they came to office in 1979. Like their policies in other areas it represents both continuities and new departures. It is probably inevitable that the new departures element would be the one emphasized by commentators and the Conservatives themselves, and be seen to represent radically new initiatives. However this is not necessarily the case. Continuities are probably stronger than radical departures in general terms. In addition it should be pointed out that not all of the Conservatives' initiatives are silly or to be unwelcome. The attempt to develop a more selective approach to investment support is a case in point. However, the Conservatives' dogmatic reluctance to conceive of an industrial policy for the economy as a whole, their over-emphasis on a small range of 'new technology' sectors, and their general lack of a serious commitment to 'competition' at the micro level present serious obstacles to their own industrial policy. 'Competition' itself is conceived in very narrow terms - rather as something emanating 'naturally' from the private ownership of economic resources. Any defence of 'competition' would need to see it confined to rather specific areas or instances within the general context of attempts at overall resources co-ordination and re-vitalization. This, then, is to place 'competition' in the political context of a different strategy than the Conservatives are likely to adopt. As it stands there seems little reason to expect that their strategy will 'solve' the major problems of a lack of dynamism in the manufacturing sector the consequences of which will begin to emerge in a much more serious form in the mid 1990s.

Notes

1. Clearly these figures are expressed in monetary totals and are not based upon volume planning. It is also well known that the 'price' of public sector inputs increases at a faster rate than the general price level (the 'Relative Price Effect') so deflating by the GDP deflator may over estimate the 'real' increase in these areas.

2. The French position was heralded as early as 1978 with the publication of the 'Nora Report' (Nora and Minc 1980). By 1982 the Japanese had already got a 'Fifth Generation' programme well under way organized through the offices of MITI (Feigenbawn and McCorduck 1984). The maverick seems to be the USA. No <u>national</u> response had emerged but it was expected that <u>IBM</u> would soon lead the way on an individual company basis.

3. All official pronouncements and the encouragements written into the White Paper and the Cable Broadcasting Bill were towards getting interactive, 'switched-star' systems (the latest technology) into the franchised areas. However 'tree and branch' systems (an older technology) would still be allowed, with only minimal interactive capability.

4. The definition of the IT industry employed by NEDO includes telecommunications, computers, office equipment and software, but it excludes semiconductors ('chips') and satellites. Including these latter two elements would have strengthened the UK industries comparative international position.

5. Interestingly enough this neglect has been less the case in the USA at least at the level of serious argument. A very lively debate about the possibilities and prospects for a comprehensive industrial policy in connection with the established US manufacturing sector has emerged in the <u>Harvard Business Review</u> since the late 1970s. See also Magaziner and Reich (1983). In the UK a number of the sectors referred to in the text are covered by various tariff and non-tariff agreements. The Conservatives have largely continued previous practice in these areas as Chapter 5 demonstrated.

References

Bagwell, P.S. (1984) <u>End of the Line</u>? Verso, London.

Brittan, S. (1984) 'The Politics and Economics of Privatization' The Political Quarterly, Vol 55 No 2 April-June pp.109-128.

CAA (1984) Airline Competition Policy : Final Report CAP 500, HMSO, London.

CSE Communications Group (1982) Hunt on Cable TV: Chaos or Coherence? The Campaign for Press and Broadcasting Freedom, London.

Devereux, M. and Mayer, C. (1984) Corporation Tax : The Impact of the 1984 Budget The Institute for Fiscal Studies, London.

Feigenbawn, E.A. and McCorduck, P. (1984) The Fifth Generation, Michael Joseph, London.

Garnham, N. (1983) 'Public Service Versus the Market' Screen, Vol 23 No 1 January-February.

Grant, W. and Wilks, S. (1982) 'Continuity and Change in Industrial Support' Public Money Vol 3 No 3 September pp.63-67.

HMSO (1982a) : A Programme for Advanced Information Technology : The Report of the Alvery Committee, HMSO, London.

HMSO (1982b) : Report on the Inquiry into Cable Expansion and Broadcasting Policy. (Hunt Committee Report) Cmnd 8679, HMSO, London.

HMSO (1983) The Development of Cable Systems and Services, Cmnd 8866, April, London.

Kay, J. and Forsythe,(1980) 'The Economic Implications of North Sea Oil Revenues' Fiscal Studies Vol 1 July pp.1-28.

King, M.A. and Fullerton, D. (1984) 'The Taxation of Income from Capital: A Comparative Study of the UK, USA, Sweden and Germany' in J. King and D. Fullerton (eds), The Taxation of Income From Capital, Chicago University Press, Chicago.

Magaziner, I. and Reich, R. (1983) Minding America's Business, Harcourt Brace, New York.

NEDO (1984a) : Crisis Facing UK Information Technology, National Economic Development Office, London.

NEDO (1984b) : Competence and Competition, National Economic Development Office, London.

Nora, S. and Minc, A. (1980) The Computerization of Society, MIT Press, London.

Northcott, J. and Rogers, P. (1984) Micro-electronics in British Industry : The Pattern of Change, Policy Studies Institute, London.

Owen, N. (1983) Economies of Scale, Competitiveness and Trade Patterns within the European Community, Clarendon Press, Oxford.

Perrakis, S. and Silva-Echenique, J. (1983) 'The

Profitability and Risk of CATV operations in Canada'. <u>Applied Economics</u> Vol 15. April pp.745-758.

Thompson, G.F. (1983) <u>Hunting the Cable : A review of the Hunt Committee Report</u>, Mimo, Open University, March.

Veljanovski, C.G. and Bishop, W.D. (1983) <u>Choice by Cable : The Economics of a New Era in Television</u>, Hobart Paper, No 96, Institute of Economic Affairs, London.

Chapter 8

CONCLUSIONS

This book has presented an interim assessment of the Conservative Government's economic strategy over the period 1979 to 1985. This is perhaps a somewhat hazardous and difficult exercise to be engaged in, in 1985, a period characterized very much by the 'mid term' feel of a strategy not yet completed. Thus an assessment 'half way through' is in danger of both expecting too much to have been accomplished, and of failing to appreciate the full extent and radicalness of the initiatives and changes actually under way. It looks as though Mrs Thatcher and her government will continue along a broadly similar course to that already pursued around the themes .of the MTFS and extensive de-regulation, for at least another three years and possibly longer. The full consequences of these are only just beginning to appear, it might be argued, and it would be wrong to underestimate their significance and effects.

However there is always a necessity to characterize as clearly as possible what is going on in the contemporary economy, and indeed an impossibility of avoiding this. The aim of this book has been to do this in as open and honest a manner as possible, though this is not to say that the sum of the criticisms and positions put forward here have been 'neutral' either in terms of economics or politically. It should at least be clear by now that the author of this book, while hostile to the intentions of the Conservatives' strategy, has aimed to cover the arguments offered on its behalf extensively and fairly.

The book has been written against a prevailing approach in these matters, which stresses the massive change in direction the Conservatives have already achieved in their management of the economy. Clearly changes have been made. This is not in dispute. But to understand the character of these requires a more serious account of the obstacles and constraints that an advanced industrialized and financially sophisticated economy, organized along capitalist lines, sets in the way of any government whatever its ideological stance or its theoretical likes and dislikes. The UK economy is set in the context of a web of international as well as domestic relationships which add to the problems of making radical initiatives in economic management. It is these obstacles and constraints that have been focussed upon in this book.

The point here is to stress the way the onset of the recession would have made it difficult for the Conservatives or anyone else to have maintained the trajectory of Post-War economic policy even if they had wanted to. In addition it is to stress how this recession provided the material conditions and groundwork on which to construct a different ideological justification for the 'change in course' that Mrs Thatcher has been so keen to celebrate. In the face of this recession there was little a small and relatively weak economy could do on its own to 'plough against the furrow' set for it by conditions largely out of its control. But as well as the recession constraining and limiting the feasible alternatives that might have been promoted by the political Left for example, it also limits what the Right and the Conservatives themselves have been able to do. The recession limits what both 'sides' might wish to achieve. This recession has been brought about by forces within capitalism that are diverse and largely outside of the competence of any single government to delay or alter. The problem this throws up for the managers of the British economy, whether from the Left or the Right of the political spectrum is to come to terms with trying to manage an economy in rather rapid relative decline. If there is a single most important lesson to be learned from the current episode it is that methods of managing economies, as well as of firms and enterprises, that have been developed in the context of growth are just not applicable in reverse when a situation of stagnation or decline sets in. Indeed one of the major ideological obstacles to overcome under these circumstances is to recognize this very fact: to appreciate that most if not all of our instruments and tools of economic intervention, management and

212

regulation have traditionally been couched in terms of a growing economy or organizational base. But trying to manage in an overt way a declining economic base requires quite a different outlook and approach as well as the development of a new set of mechanisms and practices of economic management to carry this through. A ritualistic appeal to the virtues of the 'market mechanism' as a salvation in this context is neither original enough nor to fully come to terms with the difficulties of such an enterprise. It is rather to fall back on an invocation of a golden age almost, which itself never existed in the form proposed anyway.

Much of the current discussion of the possible effects of the Conservatives' approach turns on the recession/recovery couple, with the emphasis rapidly switching to the latter aspect of this. The recovery is underway, it is suggested, and this proves the effectiveness of the Conservatives' approach. There are three responses to this. In the first place it is quite possible to argue that the recovery is not underway in anything like the form or extent suggested. Rather the economy is likely to bump along near the bottom of the cycle for some time. Forecasters are split on both the extent and the duration of the 'recovery', with strong indications that any growth response is weak though as we have seen in figure 2.3 earlier steadily advancing. Secondly, if a stronger recovery does take place in the near future the question has to be asked whether this is because of the recovery in the USA rather than because of any primary indigenous positive response on the part of the UK economy. Further to this, and connected to it is the third response which would question whether this recovery, should it eventually take place, is the result of the particular novel economic policies inaugurated by Mrs Thatcher in the UK and Mr Reagan in the US, or whether this is primarily due to a rather surrogate deployment of orthodox demand management tools (as they are termed) in both economies. The US budgetary position has already been outlined in Chapter 2 and the effects of this need little further comment other than to stress the critical necessity for the continued 'de-monetarization' of this deficit if its inflationary potential is not to reverse any US recovery altogether. In the UK context the 1984 Budget injected some £1.5 to £2 billion extra aggregate demand into the economy according to a number of calculations, largely via delaying various tax and benefit changes. Thus at this level at least it could be a somewhat orthodox set of policies that is responsible for any recovery actually underway or for such an anticipated situation when it finally arises in the future.

However there is another very non-orthodox side to the Conservatives' strategy which is not really covered by these kinds of terms and argument at all, some would argue. The technical details of this or that particular mechanism for regulating the economy misses the point of the politically and ideologically inspired attack on all things collective and socialistic. Here the Tories have changed or are changing the terrain on which the very terms for economic debate can take place and with it the characteristic practices of the economy itself. By and large this more political aspect to the Tories approach has not formed a focus for the analysis in this book, though it is not unconnected to it. It remains to be seen whether this political strategy works in the manner suggested or whether it too overemphasises the role of changes in ideological stance in producing the anticipated concrete outcomes at a more practical and day to day level.

Whatever one's position with respect to those kinds of issues, it is not controversial to recognize that the situation of the UK economy is still a very weak one. The long run decline in its international competitiveness and particularly its probable inability to sustain the present level of imports in the absence of compensating North Sea Oil revenues, is particularly problematical and worrisome. The next major 'crunch' for the economy is likely to appear in the mid 1990s as the oil revenues begin to run out. This will happen more or less independently of whichever government happens to be in power at the time. If nothing is done to re-construct the manufacturing base of the UK economy prior to this, and with it to reconstitute a serious exporting capability, the prospects for the last decade of this century look bleak indeed. As yet there is no sign that the Conservatives have the capacity to do this, or that the policies they have been deploying so far will have the desired effect. Such deep and structural problems that are thrown up in this context require genuinely innovative and fresh political and economic responses not some tired evocation of a lost past and the need to reclaim a lost purpose. The issue is not one fundamentally of individualized <u>will</u> but of the recognition of changed <u>possibilities</u>; not one of <u>initiative or incentive</u> but rather of structural <u>constraints</u> and their removal by the rendering of them in the objects of policy; not one of dogmatic <u>principle</u> but of <u>realistic and feasible alternatives</u>. The Conservatives are still beset by a dogma which celebrates the tenacity and obstinacy of individual will as heralding the changes needed in the economy. The challenge is to find a different way.

Postscript

PUBLIC EXPENDITURE IN 1984-85 AND THE MARCH 1985 BUDGET

As this book was going to press the March 1985
Budget was presented along with the Government's
public expenditure plans for 1985-86 to 1987-88.
This gives us an opportunity to bring some of the
more important figures and trends mentioned in the
main chapters up to date and to comment on the
Budget proposals in the light of the Conservatives'
overall economic strategy.

In the first place public expenditure
continued to increase in real terms over the year
1984-85 confirming the analysis offered in Chapter
2. According to the Treasury's Financial Statement
and Budget Report (HMSO 1985c), the PSBR was
forecast to be £10.5 bn in 1984-85 instead of the
targeted £7.25 bn. Thus a £3.25 bn overshot was
likely. The Chancellor attributed this to the coal
dispute. Sterling M3 growth was running at 9.5% for
1984-85 very close to the top of the target range
for this broad money indicator of 6%-10% announced
in the previous year's Budget Report.

In the White Paper on the Government's
Expenditure Plans published in January 1985 it was
reaffirmed that the Treasury's objective was to
keep its overall expenditure constant in cost terms
(HMSO 1985a). As far as public expenditure as a
percentage of GDP was concerned this stood at 42.5%
in 1984-85 on the government's own figures, exactly
the same as it had been the previous year.

But the Treasury's own expenditure figures are
notorious for disguising important trends because
definitions and coverage tend to change from one
year to the next. In the House of Commons Select
Committee report on expenditure plans a careful
comparability exercise is undertaken to make sure
one year's expenditure is properly comparable to

216

previous years. Table P.1 shows an index of total public expenditure, based upon 1983-84 prices, produced by the Committee and it confirms that public expenditure again increased in 1984-85. This table updates Table 2.2 in Chapter 2 above.

Table P.1: Index of Total Public Expenditure (1983-84 prices)

	1979-80	1983-84	1984-85
As Published	100	107.6	109.4
As Adjusted*	100	113.3	114.7

Note: * Adjusted for changes in NIS, sickness and housing benefits, special asset sales, expenditure on company securities, net purchase of land and buildings and net debt interest.

Source: HMSO (1985b) p.XII.

As far as the breakdown of expenditure on industrial support is concerned, which was discussed in Chapter 7, the White Paper for the first time produced a consolidated table of real public expenditure changes which included a separate category covering the headings 'Industry, Energy, Trade and Employment'. This simply added up the separate budgets for each of these departments. In Table P.2 the 1979-80 position on this is compared to the 1983-84 and 1984-85 totals.

Table P.2: Real Planning Totals of Government Expenditure on Industry, Energy, Trade and Employment (1979-80 to 1984-85) (£ million)

	1979-80	1983-84	% Δ on 1979-80	Expected 1984-85	% Δ on 1979-80
Expenditure	5822	5886	1%	6856	18%

Source: Drawn from HMSO (1985a) Vol II, Table 2.6, p.12.

Thus on the basis of these figures the government's real support for industry (broadly conceived) increased by only 1% between 1979-80 and 1983-84 compared to the 40% increase suggested by Table 1 Chapter 7. But the Table 7.1 calculations are both more selective and more extensive than those given in the White Paper. They are more selective in that they do not include all of the departmental expenditure which has been included in Table P.2. Rather only that part closely tied to industrial support is added in. But they are drawn more widely in that they do include other departments' specific contributions to industrial support which are excluded from the White Paper's calculations. Unfortunatley there was not the time to properly re-calculate Table 7.1 outturn 1983-84 figures and also to include 1984-85 estimated outturn figures. From Table P.2 however it can be seen that assistance to industry conceived as in the White Paper is likely to increase dramatically in 1984-85 to an 18% increase on the 1970-80 totals. A cursory survey of the details of the White Paper also confirms the general trends within the DTI's budget as discussed in Chapter 7.

In the March 1985 Budget speech itself the Chancellor, Mr Lawson, strongly reinforced the two pronged character of the Government's overall economic strategy as pointed out in Chapter 4. In fact this Budget was perhaps the first to so forcefully confirm the Government's commitment to 'supply-side' stimulation via labour market intervention, as well as to the MTFS. While the 1984 Budget looked at company taxation and other measures to stimulate investment in supply-side terms, as discussed in Chapter 7, in 1985 Mr Lawson turned his attention more explicitly to the labour market. This also strongly confirmed the ideas discussed in Chapter 6 that it is the individual's trade-off between income in work and income out of it that determines people's propensity to work. Reducing this 'replacement ratio' is supposed to increase the incentive to work. Thus the National Insurance (NI) contributions were altered in a neat attempt to both reduce the cost of employing labour from the point of view of the firm and to make the difference between income in work and out of it wider for the lower paid. In abolishing the upper earnings limit on NI contributions the Chancellor was also, in effect, making skilled labour more expensive to employ, thus presumably hoping for a substitution to cheaper labour here as well. While the Budget was seen as rather low keyed and relatively uninteresting by popular commentators in fact its significance is much greater in terms of the philosophy that informs these measures directed at the labour market. For the first time the Chancellor came out with direct measures to reduce the cost of labour and improve incentives in classic supply-side terms.

The Budget also confirmed the idea that orthodox annual budgets as such - i.e. in terms of altering government expenditure levels - have been losing their significance under Conservative administrations. The 1985 Budget was virtually neutral in aggregate demand terms. Thus 'monetarist' budgets broadly conceived need only re-affirm money supply targets and set about altering conditions on the supply-side of the economy. This changes somewhat the orthodox conception of what a budget is about. If unemployment is all 'voluntary', as was implied by the Chancellor's measures, then all governments can do to diminish unemployment is to make the incentive to work stronger. As many of the Chancellor's critics pointed out at the time however, for most unemployed people the 'choice' at the margin between being in work and being out of it is just not there. There are just no jobs available to 'choose' to go into. Here would have been a chance to stimulate the demand-side as well, in so doing opening up the possible expansion of job opportunities. But in characteristic supply-side style he chose to ignore this possibility. As a result it seems unlikely that the measures proposed will have anything but a marginal impact on unemployment.

Other supply-side measures were to increase the range of the Youth Training Schemes, effectively making them mandatory and akin to two-years National Service. Overall the wider tax changes' were likely to reduce the tax burden on the lower and upper ends of the income spectrum, probably confirming the increases in income inequality discussed in Chapter 6.

Conclusions

References

HMSO (1985a): <u>The Government's Expenditure Plans 1985-86 to 1987-88:</u> Cmnd 9428 I and II. January, HMSO, London.

HMSO (1985b): 6th Report of the Treasury and Civil Service Committee <u>The Government's Expenditure Plans 1985-86 to 1987-88:</u> HCP 213. February, HMSO, London.

HMSO (1985c): <u>Financial Statement and Budget Report 1985-86:</u> HCP 265. March, HMSO, London.

INDEX